Amy Bizzarri

111 Places in Chicago That You Must Not Miss

Photographs by Susie Inverso

emons:

© Photographs: Susie Inverso, Crimson Cat Studios, except:
3 Arts Club (ch. 1) - RH;
Alfred Caldwell Lily Pool (ch. 4) – S.P. Fargo;
Calumet Water Retention Plant (ch. 21) –
Metropolitan Water Reclamation District of Greater Chicago;
Colleen Moore Fairy Castle (ch. 32) –
Museum of Science and Industry, Chicago;
Full Moon Fire Jam (ch. 42) – Ryan Brandoff;
Maggie Daley Park Skating Ribbon (ch. 58) – Chicago Park District;
Morgan Shoal and Shipwreck (ch. 64) – Eric Allix Rogers;
Palmisano Park (ch. 76) – Robert Sit, site design group, ltd.;
Poetry Foundation (ch. 80) – Heinrich Blessing;
Signature Room Loo (ch. 90) – The Signature Room at the 95th®
Design: Eva Kraskes, based on a design
by Lübbeke | Naumann | Thoben
Edited by Karen E. Seiger
Maps: altancicek.design, www.altancicek.de
Printing and binding: Grafisches Centrum Cuno, Calbe
Printed in Germany 2020
ISBN 978-3-7408-1030-6
5th edition, March 2020

Foreword

Flying into Chicago at night over the vast, dark blue Lake Michigan, stars twinkling above, I hear Liz Phair's "Stratford-on-Guy" musings on returning home. From above, Chicago is peaceful, "lit from within," with its grid glowing amber. Covered with a blanket of freshly fallen snow, it is magical.

Chicago's seasons give us an edge. Long, cold winters make us strong. You can't call yourself a true Chicagoan until you've shoveled your car out of an alley packed with snow. Spring fills us up with flowers. They don't call us *Urbs in Horto* – City in a Garden – for nothing. Come summertime, we cherish our lakefront, chill over beer and BBQ, and cheer on the Cubs, our lovable losers. We don't give up. On anyone. Fall sees our trees dressed up in fiery red hues that recall the Great Fire of October 1871. This is a city that excels at rising from the ashes.

Here are the 111 off-the-radar places that conjure up the hard-working, inventive soul of Chicago: from the venues where music lifts us, including a mom-and-son-owned blues lounge and a thirties-era piano lounge hidden in an apartment building, to the places where we gather to place bets on racing turtles, fill our bellies with Chicago-style hot dogs, or welcome the full moon with a jam session on the beach. If you're looking for a little dose of Chicago's magic, snorkel the South Side limestone shelf that teems with life, or sip champagne from the clandestine cupola atop a Beaux Arts skyscraper. Every place highlights Chicago's ability to transform, rapidly and creatively: potholes morph into mosaics; vacant lots into apiaries; and industrial wastelands into serene spaces where wild creatures come to play.

Walking through the city that Sarah Bernhardt once christened "the pulse of America," I am reminded that it is Chicago's no-nonsense, broad-shouldered citizens who make it feel like home.

Welcome to my Windy City.

Amy Bizzarri

111 Places

1 3 Arts Club Courtyard

A room of her own

In its almost 100-year history, the 3 Arts Club of Chicago served as a safe, supportive, and economical residence for over 13,000 young women as they studied the "three arts": music, painting, and drama. Founded in 1912 by social work pioneer Jane Addams and 30 other women from some of Chicago's wealthiest families, including social activist Edith Rockefeller McCormick, the club financed this beautiful, Byzantine building on swanky Dearborn Street with the goal of providing each resident, all promising young, female artists, with a room of her own as well as a chance to meet and collaborate with other artists in the same circumstances, all new to the city and working to find their way in the world of the arts.

Designed by Holabird and Roche, the building opened its arched main doors in 1914, and was complete with all the trappings of an artist's retreat within the big city: a library, tearoom, studio space, dining room, and three floors of dormitory rooms centered on a spacious, inspiring open courtyard.

The club provided the young women living there with both independence and security. The last residents moved out in 2004, and the building stood closed and unused until 2015, when Restoration Hardware moved into the 70,000-square-foot landmark build, and transformed it into a six-floor spectacle of a furniture store that feels like a museum. The grand staircase that once ushered up-and-coming artists out onto the town, a rooftop conservatory with stunning views of the Gold Coast, and a historic stage glittering with gilded mirrors – all were lovingly restored back to life after being shuttered for years.

The crown jewel is the courtyard, open year-round thanks to a new pyramid of glass and steel, with the grandest chandelier in the city of Chicago dripping from the pyramidion. Settle in for a northern-California-inspired menu and you'll be bathed in sunshine and surrounded by flowers, olive trees, and topiaries.

Address 1300 N Dearborn Parkway, Chicago, IL 60610, +1 (312) 475-9116 | Getting there Subway to Clark/Division (Red Line) | Hours Mon–Sat 10am–8pm; Sun 11am–6pm | Tip There is usually a wait for a table in the courtyard, so make the most of it by ordering a Bellini or a flute of fine champagne from the rear espresso counter, and head to the rooftop garden, where you can sip while enjoying the gorgeous views.

2 The 606

Chicago's elevated escape

The 606, a 2.7-mile trail that connects four ground-level parks and four amazing Chicago neighborhoods, is set high above the city streets, on tall, steel-reinforced concrete embankments that once carried train tracks. Running eastward along Bloomingdale Avenue, from Ashland Avenue towards Ridgeway Avenue to the west, this glorious stretch of green space offers a bird's-eye view into Chicago city life.

The elevated Bloomingdale Line was built in 1915 to prevent freight trains from killing pedestrians at street-level crossings. Thirty-eight viaducts, still in place today, allowed passersby to make their way safely beneath the rails. In time, trucks began to replace trains, and the last freight cars made their way down from the line in 2001. Weeds took over the tracks, and the elevated line was closed to the public.

In the early 2000s, a grassroots organization dreamed up a plan for the neglected rail line. Smooth, wide pavement replaced the rails; colorful native prairie flowers replaced weeds. Runners, walkers, bikers, and nature lovers of all ages replaced trains. Today, kids learn to ride bicycles here; commuters use the trail as a shortcut to work; lovers walk into the sunset together. Vibrant art installations and dynamic, creative programming make each visit to the 606 different from the last.

The elevated 606 is an escape from the city that intersects the city, a place to catch your breath and see Chicago from a new perspective. Since it stands almost 20 feet above the streets, one can peer into the many windows that line the trail and look out over the city of Chicago, with a clear, sweeping view of its skyscraping skyline in the distance. The new trailway was named in honor of the zip code prefix – 606 – for the diverse neighborhoods that are now connected, not only by the three digits but also by this remarkable urban oasis.

Address Bloomingdale Avenue, from Ashland Avenue on the east to Ridgeway Avenue on the west, www.the606.org | Getting there There are 12 access points to the 606; visit the website for addresses and an interactive map | Hours Daily dawn–dusk | Tip Though you can always walk the length of the trail, renting a Divvy bike is the easy and fun way to explore the 606. There are 17 Divvy bike rental stations located within a block of the 606. Your best bet is to enter the trail at the Julia de Burgos Park access point, where you'll also find a Divvy station (1805 N Albany Avenue, www.divvybikes.com).

3 Al Capone's Booth

Rhapsody in Green

Even though he owned a speakeasy in the basement across the street, gangster extraordinaire Al Capone loved the Green Mill Cocktail Lounge above all. When Scarface entered, the bandleader knew it was best to pause everything and play "Rhapsody in Blue" – pronto! From his favorite moss green, velvet-lined booth, directly across from the side-door entrance on Lawrence, near the end of the bar, Chicago's Big Fellow, as his criminal associates called him, could assess whoever entered the bar while simultaneously soaking in whatever act was onstage.

Capone's favorite crooner in the twenties was Joe E. Lewis. In 1927, Lewis was "asked" to sign a contract that required him to sing exclusively at the Green Mill, at the request of Jack "Machine Gun" McGurn, a mobster pal of Capone. When he refused, he was bludgeoned with a revolver, and his throat and tongue slashed with a hunting knife. Amazingly, he survived the attack and returned to perform as a comic at the Green Mill; McGurn went on to mastermind the Saint Valentine's Day Massacre. The Green Mill tells this story in part, on the large wood carving above the bar, which depicts the cast of characters and poetically sets the scene with the inscription: "Big Al was ingesting spaghetti / Machine Gun McGurn strangely still / Told Joe E., 'You'll look like confetti / If you try to quit the Green Mill.'"

If the walls of the Green Mill could talk, they'd have so many soulful stories to tell. From the jazz greats – Billie Holiday, Von Freeman, Wilbur Campbell, Kurt Elling, Orbert Davis – who mesmerized audiences in the once smoke-filled lounge, to the mobsters and movie stars who mingled over martinis in this timeless jazz bar, the Green Mill is haunted with legends of long ago. For over 100 years Ceres, Goddess of Harvest, has watched over the crowds in this Art Deco gem, the best jazz club in Chicago, and likely the world.

Address 4802 N Broadway, Chicago, IL 60640, +1 (773) 878-5552, www.greenmilljazz.com | Getting there Subway to Lawrence (Red Line) | Hours Mon–Fri noon–4am; Sat noon–5am; Sun 11am–4am | Tip You can still catch great jazz at the Green Mill – as well as great poetry. Every Sunday night, 7pm–10pm, poets sling poems on the Green Mill's stage during the interactive Uptown Poetry Slam, the longest running slam in the city.

4 Alfred Caldwell Lily Pool

Chicago's Prairie-style oasis

Tucked in a gated corner of Lincoln Park, the wild yet intimate Alfred Caldwell Lily Pool is easy to miss. It is a timeless, hidden oasis that promises a moment of peace in the middle of a city on the move.

Designed by renowned architect Alfred Caldwell, the pool's landscape recalls a lush, Illinois River valley dotted with wild flowers. Follow the stonework path that meanders along the lily-spotted lagoon, through the native-plant-filled landscape, and past the gurgling waterfall; ascend the stone steps to the circular council ring that overlooks the pond and offers a glimpse of Lake Michigan. This is perhaps the best spot in the city to relax and reflect.

Originally built in 1889 as an ornate, Victorian-style garden, the artificially-heated lily pool became home to frogs and invasive plants that soon undermined the intended, romantic feel. In 1936, Alfred Caldwell was hired by the Works Progress Administration to recover the overgrown, neglected garden. He strived to create a natural, Midwestern ecosystem contained within 2.7 acres in Lincoln Park. When the city park district cut the project budget, Caldwell was so set on his poetic plan that he cashed in his $5,000 life insurance policy for $250 and bought thousands of native plants from Sauk County, Wisconsin, planting them, together with his crew, the very next day. The result is an ode to the Midwest before the Europeans set foot on the river plains.

By the 1950s, migratory birds had claimed the gated getaway as a rookery of their very own, and the Lincoln Park Zoo followed their cue, transforming it into an avian exhibit. Before long, the birds and weeds took over, leading to further erosion. It wasn't until the Lincoln Park Conservancy stepped in that the landscape was restored to Caldwell's original vision, and the lily pool, a glorious example of Prairie-style landscape architecture, reopened in 2002.

Address 125 W Fullerton Parkway, Chicago, IL 60614, +1 (773) 883-7275, www.lincolnparkconservancy.org | Getting there CTA bus 151 to Stockton & Arlington or CTA bus 22 to Clark & Fullerton | Hours Daily 7:30am–7pm | Tip Built in the late 1890s to showcase exotic plants and flowers in a city that was rapidly industrializing, the nearby Lincoln Park Conservatory is an exotic-style Victorian-era glasshouse garden. A 50-foot-tall fiddle-leaf rubber tree, planted in 1891, still thrives in the lush Palm House (2391 N Stockton Drive, www.chicagoparkdistrict.com/parks).

5 Aloft Loft Circus Arts

A sanctuary for circus arts

In an historic 109-year-old church in the heart of Logan Square, acrobatics have replaced altars; poles, prayers; balancers, bibles; and clown arts, catechism. Light still streams in through the colorful stained glass windows. But instead of shining upon parishioners, the sun's rays illuminate artists twirling and swirling on 40-foot-long ropes suspended from the ultra-high vaulted ceiling. Aspiring circus artists are the new parishioners at the former First Evangelical Church on Wrightwood Avenue, ever since Aloft Circus took over the building in 2016, making this sanctuary the top spot in the city to learn the art of the trapeze, trampoline, tight-wire and more.

The challenging and fun classes here are open to both professional performers and aspiring amateurs, and small class sizes mean more time up in the air. The Full Time Training Program is the country's only two-contiguous-year professional track program, with 40 hours per week of training dedicated to creating skillful and heartfelt circus graduate professionals. Introductory classes in everything from Cyr wheel spinning to clowning are open to anyone with a bit of courage, a grand sense of play, and, most importantly, an endless sense of humor.

All the instruction takes place in Aloft's 6,000-square-foot main congregation area, making for a collaborative learning experience. It is common to see several acts in progress at once in this always bustling space: clowns practicing their best juggling moves beside balancing acrobats, while tightrope walkers float overhead. Aloft Circus bought the church for about $1 million, raising an additional $60,000 through a crowdfunding campaign, making this a community-fueled project that led to the third largest circus school in the country.

Aloft excels in helping to build confidence and strength while upping life's fun factor, all clowning aside.

Address 3324 W Wrightwood Avenue, Chicago, IL 60647, +1 (773) 782-6662, www.aloftloft.com | Getting there Subway to Logan Square (Blue Line) | Hours Check website for class schedule. | Tip Go see Sanctuary, Aloft's monthly circus cabaret show, hosted the first Saturday evening of every month. Tickets and more info at www.aloftloft.com.

6 American Science & Surplus

Everything you didn't know you needed

Whether you're looking to create the best new Autobot, need a life-size bat skeleton immediately, or want to stock up on 24-inch military-grade suction cups, you'll find everything you didn't know you needed, and more, at American Science & Surplus. This Chicago-based company has been serving the scientific community for over 75 years with its unbeatable selection of weird, wacky, multi-purpose stuff, and objects with purposes unknown.

As purveyors of the quirky, quaint, and quintessential, American Science & Surplus goes above and beyond, to stock their shelves with the extraordinary. Where else can you find rubber chickens sitting on a shelf between a tub of arcade button switches and foot-long tailors' shears? A portable two-person military latrine? An eight-foot diameter weather balloon? A plush pig with a fish bowl belly? A 3-foot tall polyresin iguana? A foldable frying pan? This is Chicago's most bizarre bazaar, so plan on spending at least an hour treasure hunting.

As the story goes, founder Al Luebbers came across a pile of reject industrial lenses that a company, next door to the plant where he worked, was throwing away. He inquired about the reject items, and got them for nothing as long as he would haul them away. Realizing he could resell odds and ends for a profit, Luebbers opened American Science & Surplus in the late 1930s, and he's been hauling away rejects ever since. To this day, closeouts, inventory overruns, mismanufactures, and items whose time has not yet come find their way to the shelves at this browseworthy store.

A word of warning: if you see something that piques your curiosity, buy it today, because it likely won't be available tomorrow. When it's gone, it's gone. But a new treasure will show up in its place.

Address 5316 N Milwaukee Avenue, Chicago, IL 60630, +1 (773) 763-0313, www.sciplus.com | Getting there Subway to Gladstone (Blue Line) | Hours Mon–Wed 10am–7pm; Thu 10am–8pm; Fri 10am–7pm; Sat 10am–6pm; Sun 11am–5pm | Tip Use your nose to track the garlicky scent of *kielbasa* fresh from the smoker at Andy's Deli and Mikolajczyk Sausage Shop Inc., located two blocks south of American Science & Surplus. More than two dozen kinds of delectable, house-made sausages hang on the walls of this revered Polish-American deli, all made onsite the Old World way. Add freshly baked breads and rolls as well as a fine selection of house-prepared Polish delights to your basket for a lunch fit for a king (5442 N Milwaukee Avenue).

7 Aragon Ballroom

Musical milestones under Mediterranean skies

Supernatural musical experiences are commonplace under the Aragon Ballroom's ever-twinkling lights. Grunge band Nirvana played their final show here, performing the long-bootlegged, beloved song "You Know You're Right." Green Day filmed their *MTV Jaded in Chicago* concert to a sell-out crowd here; funk metal band Primus filmed their first concert DVD, *Hallucino-Genetics*, from the Aragon's stage; sludge metal band Mastodon recorded a live album and concert DVD on a typically wild Aragon night.

Soon after it opened in 1926, the Aragon was flooded with music-loving Chicagoans. They came via the L, which was packed to capacity on every night of the six-day business week. Hit station WGN broadcast live from the Aragon, furthering its appeal among the young and musically inclined. Newspaper advertisements for the ballroom vaunted "visions of languorous *señoritas* and dashing *caballeros*" and "moon-drenched patios and stately turrets gently brushing Mediterranean skies." A postcard from the era boasted, "He Who Has Not Been At Aragon Knows Not What A Paradise It Is!"

Legend has it that secret tunnels leading from the Aragon's basement to the nearby Green Mill bar provided an easy escape for music-loving mobsters. Al Capone sat in his private, southwest balcony booth where a fire escape guaranteed an easy exit. The ballroom's basement doubled as a speakeasy, run by bootlegging king Hymie Weiss and the gang of Charles "Deanie" O' Banion, a Capone rival who was later gunned down while clipping chrysanthemums in his family-run floral shop.

In the sixties the Aragon morphed into a mod discotheque; in the seventies it became the home of monster rock marathons, earning it the nickname the "Aragon Brawlroom." Today, you'll find an eclectic calendar of concerts featuring just about every genre of music you can imagine, from rap to reggaeton.

Address 1106 W Lawrence Avenue, Chicago, IL 60640, +1 (773) 561-9500, www.aragonballroom.org | Getting there Subway to Lawrence (Red Line) | Hours Check website for schedule. | Tip The nearby Uptown Theatre stands as the last of the "big three" movie palaces built by the Balaban & Katz theatre chain. Though it's closed to the public while it undergoes an extensive restoration, you can still peek in the main doors of its grand, eight-story façade to view the opulent five-story entrance lobby, which you might recognize from *Transformers 4* (4816 N Broadway, www.uptowntheatre.com).

8_Ardis Krainik Backstage

Where theatrical magic really happens

The Lyric Opera specializes in harnessing the power of costume, scenery, lighting, sound effects, and above all, movement, music, and voice to carry audience members to altogether new places, periods, and heights. As an epic opera unfolds onstage, it is easy to find yourself suddenly transported to the lively Latin Quarter of Paris, to a soldier-filled square in Seville, or to 19th-century Calabria, among a traveling troupe of clowns.

Housed in the historic Civic Opera House, the Lyric's Ardis Krainik Theatre is the second-largest opera auditorium in North America, and an Art Nouveau gem. It has ushered in all the icons of opera, including Rudolph Nureyev, Maria Callas, Luciano Pavarotti, and Plácido Domingo. But the real magic takes place backstage.

Once per month, the Lyric unveils its backstage secrets, with private tours available upon request. Two-hour, ten-stop walking tours are guided by professional staff and trained volunteers. Experts will be on hand to share insider tips in the various staging areas that are usually off-limits to the general public.

On a guided backstage tour, you will journey to the heart of the Lyric, starting in the orchestra pit, and then venturing beneath the stage to see the machinery used for trapdoor and lift elements in action. In the wardrobe department, hundreds of drawings demand to be brought to life in luxe antique fabric. Over 15,000 costumes, some over 100 years old, wait patiently to be worn during the new season. In the wig department, seven full-time staff members use tiny crochet hooks to craft ornate wigs out of yak hair. Look into the star-studded mirror in the make-up department and choose your disguise from the many prosthetics. Test your fear of heights as you stroll the sixth-floor catwalk.

You will leave with a completely new understanding and appreciation of the wizardry that takes place behind the scenes.

Address 20 N Upper Wacker Drive, Chicago, IL 60606, +1 (312) 827-5600, www.lyricopera.org | **Getting there** Subway to Washington/Wells (Brown, Orange, Pink, and Purple Line) | **Tip** The Civic Opera House's elegant Sarah and Peer Pedersen Room is where ticketholders in the know dine pre-performance. Located on the main floor, the gorgeous room offers reasonable fixed-price lunch and dinner options. You can also pre-order desserts and cocktails and they'll be waiting for you during the intermission or post-performance.

9 Architectural Artifacts

Home of almost-lost treasures

Designers, collectors, and home decorators looking for truly unique, always interesting, and sometimes outrageous museum-quality furnishings know to go directly to Architectural Artifacts. Where else can you find a pair of 20,000 pound, monumental, carved limestone horses that once served as gateside sentinels at an historic horse farm in Barrington, Illinois? Or an oversized Italian cabinet, c.1930, by Meroni and Fossati, from the Terme di Salsomaggiore, an ancient Roman spa outside Parma, Italy? Or four different seven-foot zodiac clock faces from the original Schlitz brewery in Milwaukee, Wisconsin?

Located in a former factory complex in historic Ravenswood, Architectural Artifacts is comprised of two buildings bridged by catwalks and a soaring atrium. Stone columns, statuary, gazebos, garden furniture and planters fill the spacious outdoor courtyard. The space is so captivating with its glimmering treasures that it has become a popular wedding venue, after hours.

For over 25 years, owner Stuart Grannen, a modern-day Indiana Jones with an eye for detail, has been filling this 80,000-square-foot, five-level warehouse with his salvaged finds, gathered from Chicago and beyond. "It's a treasure hunt every single day," declares Grannen, who has traveled to the far reaches of the globe in search of architectural gems about to be lost forever.

The most precious items in the ever-evolving collection recall Chicago of days gone by. When old city buildings face the wrecking ball, it's Grannen who goes in and gathers the jewels before they're lost to modernization. On one particular day, the inventory included a remarkable pair of iron elevator doors from Adler & Sullivan's Chicago Stock Exchange building (c.1893; demolished 1972), a rare leaded stained glass panel from a Lake Shore Drive penthouse, and a pair of arched top doors from the historic Morse House in Glencoe.

Address 4325 N Ravenswood Avenue, Chicago, IL 60613, +1 (773) 348-0622, www.architecturalartifacts.com | **Getting there** Subway to Montrose (Brown Line) | **Hours** Daily 10am–5pm | **Tip** Rebuilding Exchange is another great Chicago salvage resource for DIY enthusiasts. The goods here are neither as rare nor as old, but they include reclaimed appliances, cabinetry, doors, windows, and wood beams that still have a history, and make for unique and green home decor (1740 W Webster Avenue, www.rebuildingexchange.org).

10__Athenian Candle

Tradition hand-dipped with love

Athenian Candle's beautiful lambathes, traditional Orthodox candles, have been the glowing light source for thousands upon thousands of weddings, baptisms, and religious holidays in Chicago's Near West Side Greek community for almost 100 years. Since it was founded in 1922, this family-owned cornerstone business has been making the cherished tapered candles in-house and with love.

Chicago's Greektown is centered on a bustling, four-block stretch of Halsted Street that runs from Madison to Van Buren. Themistocles Godelas, a candle maker in Greece, and his wife, Efthimia, founded Athenian Candle in 1922 on the corner of West Jackson, at the center of the Halsted action, not long after they immigrated to Chicago from Athens.

The lambathes at Athenian Candle are made of pure beeswax and recognized for their romantic, soft glow and smokeless, slow burn. Hand-dipped one paper-thin layer at a time, twelve to twenty-nine times, they come in sizes that vary from eight to sixty inches in height. These candles are central to Greek Orthodox ceremonies. For baptisms, children circle the font three times, carrying smaller lambathes. Brides and grooms each hold lighted candles during the traditional wedding ceremony.

In addition to their iconic lambathes, Athenian Candle carries oil lamps (kandilia), worry beads (komboloi) and wedding crowns (stefana). Tamas, small silver rectangles embossed with just about every ailing body part you can imagine, are ready to be whisked away to altars near and far as offerings for urgent health-related prayer requests.

Interestingly, the shop also carries a wide selection of spirit candles that promises to rid you of your money woes, find you a good husband or tame a terrible one, ban bad sprits from your home, and more. Ritualistic aerosol sprays will allegedly not only extinguish undesirable odors but also clear your psychic energy field.

Address 4300 S Halsted Street, Chicago, IL 60661, +1 (312) 332-6988, www.atheniancandle.com | **Getting there** Subway to UIC/Halsted (Blue Line) | **Hours** Mon–Tue & Fri 9:30am–6pm, Thu 9:30am–7pm, Sat 9:30am–5pm | **Tip** The National Hellenic Museum's Frank S. Kamberos Oral History Project is the largest national effort to record the Greek immigrant experience in America by interviewing and recording the life stories of Americans of Greek origin. Listen to the tales or record your own at the kiosk located in the permanent Greek Story in America exhibit (333 S Halsted Street, www.nationalhellenicmuseum.org).

11 Beer Baron Row

Brewing their fortunes

At the center of Chicago's eclectic Wicker Park neighborhood lies the eponymous triangular-shaped park that early developer Charles Wicker and his brother Joel donated to the city in 1870. After the Great Chicago Fire, the duo laid plans for a subdivision, with a mix of lot sizes, on their newly purchased 80 acres of land along Milwaukee Avenue. They made their fortune from homeless Chicagoans who had lost everything in the fire, and who were now looking westward to rebuild their houses and their lives.

Among Chicago's wealthy Northern European, beer-loving immigrants were the brewers themselves, who worked hard to rise from the ashes and reestablish their breweries. They made Wicker Park a neighborhood of their very own, building ornate Victorian mansions on the tree-lined streets, particularly Hoyne and Pierce Avenues, which became known as Beer Baron Row.

At 2137 W Pierce Avenue is the gingerbread-style mansion of German-American furniture tycoon Hermann Weinhardt. Across the street, the house at 2138 W Pierce Avenue, which once served as the Polish Consulate, features elaborate exterior Stick-Eastlake-style decorative wood carvings – the original owner was treasurer of a wood-milling company. Famed pianist Ignacy Paderewski once gave an outdoor concert from the veranda, and it has been known as the Paderewski House ever since. The Italianate dream of a mansion at 1407 N Hoyne Avenue is thought to be haunted: the original owner, German wine and beer merchant John H. Rapp, was murdered here by his bookkeeper.

1558 N Hoyne Street is one of the oldest homes in the area, having been built in 1877 for C. Hermann Plautz, founder of the Chicago Drug and Chemical Company. The metal exterior trim, a post-fire precaution, is worth noting. The real cannon displayed on the lawn remains from the years when the home served as an American Legion Hall.

Address N Hoyne Avenue & W Pierce Avenue, Chicago, IL 60622 | Getting there Subway to Damen (Blue Line) | Tip Many scenes from the 2000 hit movie *High Fidelity* were filmed in buildings along Wicker Park's stretch of Milwaukee Avenue, including the former Double Door venue (1572 N Milwaukee Avenue) and the fictional record store Championship Vinyl (1500 N Milwaukee Avenue).

12 Beyond the Vines

Where diehard Cubs fans rest in peace

The Chicago Cubs, affectionately known as "the Lovable Losers" for a very long time, seemed destined to remain Major League Baseball's underdogs for all eternity. Though the team won back-to-back World Series championships in 1907 and 1908, and appeared in seven World Series following their 1908 title, most recently in 1945, their 108-year-long losing streak seemed unbreakable. But the strong fan base never gave up on their beloved Cubbies, and in 2016, when the Chicago Cubs beat out the Cleveland Indians to clench the World Series title, after a century-long-plus wait, long-suffering Cubs fans wept tears of joy, burst into cheers and swarmed into the streets surrounding Wrigley Field. Once you're a Cubs fan, you're a Cubs fan forever.

At Bohemian National Cemetery, the most vehement Cubs fans can celebrate their beloved team's most recent victory and all future ones, even in the afterlife. The cemetery's "Beyond the Vines" Columbarium offers deceased Cubs fans the chance to be buried in an urn set inside a 24-foot-high brick wall covered with ivy, just like the famous and beloved ivy-covered outfield wall at Chicago's Wrigley Field.

The Cubbie Columbarium was the brilliant idea of Dennis Mascari, who, after paying a visit to the cemetery, decided that there had to be a better, happier backdrop beyond boring old gravestones for fans of the baseball club. The wall may seem a little creepy, but not to Cubs fans. Mascari himself was interred in one of its "Eternal Skyboxes" in 2011.

A stained glass scoreboard, a small patch of Wrigley turf and a bench reportedly used in the Cubs bullpen all provide the deceased yet die-hard fans who are buried here with the chance to spend eternity with the field that brought them so much joy during their lifetimes. Ballpark seats invite visitors to remember happier times, watching games unfold with their lost loved ones.

Address Bohemian National Cemetery, 5255 N Pulaski Road, Chicago, IL 60630, +1 (773) 539-8442, www.friendsofbnc.org | **Getting there** Subway to Irving Park (Blue Line) then CTA bus 53 to Pulaski & Foster | **Hours** Daily 7:30am–5pm | **Tip** Chicago Mayor Anton Cermak, who was assassinated in 1933 when he took a bullet intended for President Franklin Roosevelt, is buried in an Art Deco-style mausoleum at Bohemian National Cemetery. Inscribed on the marble enclosing the tomb are the famous last words Cermak spoke to Roosevelt: "I'm glad it was me instead of you."

13_Big Monster Door

Beware of the hairy green monster

Chicago has long been a toy-making town. Many of the great classics were manufactured here, from Lincoln Logs to Tinkertoys. Beyond manufacturing these delights, Chicago excels at dreaming them up, and many of the most beloved (and successful) toys and games of the 20th century were invented here, including Mr. Machine, Lite Brite, Ants in the Pants, Operation, Mystery Date and Simon. Though few manufacturers remain today, one game and toy creating company, Big Monster Toys, keeps the fun in the city, thanks to their unique door, a brilliant reminder of the joy of toys.

If you happen to be walking down Racine Avenue in the Near West Side, don't be alarmed if you spot a big, hairy, green monster staring through the windowpane of a gigantic door. Approach the door slowly and cautiously, and your perspective of the world will be magically altered - a truly *Alice in Wonderland* experience (and a great Instagram moment), see if you can jump up and grab the monster-sized doorknob.

The oh-so-scary monster is on guard to protect the top-secret toy-making shenanigans that happen behind the scenes on the other side of this door – the closest you'll ever get to Santa's Workshop. Big Monster Toys designs, engineers, and prototypes toys and games for big names in the toy biz – Mattel, Moose, Fisher Price, and Hasbro to name a few. Fashion Polly Pocket, My Size Barbie, Uno Attack, Bulls-Eye Ball, and Hot Wheels Criss Cross Crash were all birthed here, behind this giant door.

The creative company was founded in 1988 when former associates of the legendary Chicago-based toy design firm Marvin Glass & Associates joined forces to create Breslow, Morrison, Terzian, & Associates, a.k.a. BMT, which later became known as Big Monster Toys. Chances are you or your kids have played with a toy that grew out of the minds of some of the non-monsters who work in this playful building.

Address 21 S Racine Avenue, Chicago, IL 60607, +1 (312) 829-8679, www.bmttoys.com | Getting there Subway to Racine (Blue Line) or Morgan (Green Line) | Tip You'll find a monster-sized red wagon just outside the HQ of Radio Flyer, yet another iconic Chicago-based toy company, founded in 1917 (6515 W Grand Avenue, www.radioflyer.com).

14 Biograph Theater

Public Enemy No. 1 meets his maker

On a sweltering summer evening, July 22, 1934, a slick gangster wearing a pinstriped suit and a snazzy straw hat settled into his seat at the air-conditioned Biograph Theater, his two girlfriends snuggled by his side, to catch the latest Clark Gable flick, Manhattan Melodrama. This wasn't your everyday Chicago gangster's night out: this dapper gentleman had killed a police officer, robbed 24 banks and four police stations, and escaped from jail twice. He had somehow managed to evade police in four states for almost a year, even undergoing underground plastic surgery to alter his appearance, and was hiding out in a North Side brothel. But little did Public Enemy No. 1, John Herbert Dillinger, know, as the credits rolled, that in minutes he would meet his maker under the glow of the Biograph's marquee lights.

At the height of the Depression, Dillinger was considered the most notorious of all outlaws. He was the much sought-after nemesis of FBI Director J. Edgar Hoover, who developed a more sophisticated FBI in response to the unparalleled bravado of Dillinger and his crew.

Ultimately betrayed by his weakness for women, it was one of the gals sitting by his side, the Romanian-born Ana Sage, a.k.a. "The Woman in Red," who tipped off the agents in return for coveted permanent U.S. residency. As Dillinger exited the Biograph, arm-in-arm with his two ladies, federal agents swooped in to make the arrest. Dillinger drew his Colt Model 1908 Vest Pocket and attempted to flee as he had managed to do so many times in the past. Instead he was met with a hailstorm of bullets, and was killed on the spot. For ten days after his death, thousands of skeptical spectators lined up to view his body at the Cook County morgue.

After 90 years as a movie theater, the Biograph was purchased as the new live theater performance venue for the Victory Gardens Playwrights Ensemble in 2004.

Address 2433 N Lincoln Avenue, Chicago, IL 60614, +1 (773) 871-3000, www.victorygardens.org | Getting there Subway to Fullerton (Brown, Purple, and Red Line) | Hours Check website for show times and tickets. | Tip Show your Victory Gardens tickets for discounts at Sedgwick's Bar & Grill, Tandoor Char House, the Twisted Baker, and several other nearby establishments for pre- or post-theater refreshments (www.victorygarden.com/plan-your-visit/area-dining).

15 Body Slices

Look through a Plexiglas tomb

Imagine walking down a dark stairwell and suddenly encountering two cadavers, each cut into multiple half-inch-thick slices that have been pressed within sheets of clear Plexiglas. For years, these gruesome body slices were hidden in a poorly lit stairwell, spooking little children who happened to come across them by chance. Parents, equally disturbed, were then forced to answer question after question from their wide-eyed kids: "Are they really real dead people?" "Who sliced them up?" "Why?" And yet these objects were not a sensation in a haunted house. The freaky yet fascinating body slices were kept hidden away for many years at Chicago's renowned Museum of Science and Industry, also known as MSI.

Who were these sad souls who forewent resting in peace for an eternity of creeping out children from within their transparent Plexiglas tombs?

The two bodies were actually those of donors to a doctor who worked at what is now Michael Reese Hospital in the late 1920s, and their carefully sliced bodies were first put on display in the Century of Progress Exposition at the 1933 World's Fair, before being loaned by the doctor to the newly opened MSI. They were placed in the Blue Stairwell, where they always appeared to be on the brink of oozing out of their Plexiglas encasing, and escaping towards a proper burial.

Instead, the infamous body slices joined up with their more modern friends – bodies meticulously preserved using special plastics and a technique called "plastination" – as part of MSI's dramatic health and wellness exhibit, YOU! The Experience. Though in many ways the exhibit is a cemetery of sorts, the focus is on personal health and well-being, and the extraordinary workings of our bodies.

All of the slices and specimens were voluntarily donated by individuals who willed that, upon their death, their bodies should be used for the education of others.

Address Museum of Science and Industry, 5700 S Lake Shore Drive, Chicago, IL 60637, +1 (773) 684-1414, www.msichicago.org | Getting there Train to 55th-56th-57th Street (Metra Electric and South Shore Line) | Hours Daily 9:30am–4pm; check website for extended hours and exceptions | Tip In a small, darkened gallery near the YOU! The Experience exhibit, 24 real human embryos and fetuses, ranging from 28 days to 38 weeks, are suspended in time as part of the Prenatal Development Collection. All allegedly failed to survive because of accidents or natural causes. They were collected in the 1930s by a certain Dr. Helen Button.

16 Brunk Children's Museum of Immigration

Welcome, step aboard a steamship to America

Would you leave home today in search of a better tomorrow? Imagine saying goodbye to the life you know, sailing away in steerage on a steamship, and setting foot onto a new, promised land, where a new language, culture, and plenty of hard work await. The Brunk Children's Museum of Immigration bridges past and present, giving children a small taste of the challenging lives of the immigrants that built Chicago.

It is hard to believe that at one time there were more Swedes in Chicago than in any city outside of Stockholm. In the late 1800s, the Swedish-born population in Chicago increased by roughly 233 percent, and by 1930 there were 65,735 Swedish-born Chicagoans and more than 140,000 children of Swedish immigrants settled in Chicago. Most settled in the North Side neighborhood of Andersonville, the heart of which is considered the corner of Clark Street and Berwyn Avenue, where you'll find the Brunk Children's Museum of Immigration housed within the Swedish American Museum.

Kids at this strictly hands-on museum enter Old World Sweden first, where a traditional Scandinavian red *stuga* house and many farm chores await. Then it's time to pack their belongings in a trunk and make the move to the New World, via the replica 20-foot steamship. Upon arrival in America, kids can settle into a pioneer log cabin and get to work milking the cow, farming a small plot of land, setting the table for dinner, bringing in firewood and more.

Be sure to check out the Swedish American Museum's permanent exhibit, The Dream of America: Swedish Immigration to Chicago. Members of the Andersonville community shared precious family keepsakes, including passports, handcrafted heirlooms and steamship tickets to bring this community-sourced exhibit to life.

Address 5211 N Clark Street, Chicago, IL 60640, +1 (773) 728-8111, www.swedishamericanmuseum.org | Getting there Subway to Berwyn (Red Line) | Hours Mon–Thu 1–4pm; Fri 10am–4pm; Sat & Sun 11am–4pm | Tip Simon's Tavern is Chicago's unofficial Swedish outpost, a dive bar with Viking decor and shiplike ambiance thanks to a bar modeled after a French steamship (5210 N Clark Street, +1 (773) 878-0894).

17_Bubbly Creek

Reclaiming nature from the Jungle

In the early 20th century, the pristine South Fork of the Chicago River morphed into an open sewer for the Union Stock Yards. Meatpackers dumped so much blood, entrails and offal into what was once a serene wetland that it began to bubble with methane and hydrogen sulfide gas; its banks were coated in animal hair and waste.

It was so polluted that in 1906, author Upton Sinclair wrote in *The Jungle*, his expose on Chicago's meatpacking industry, "… the filth stays there forever and a day … bubbles of carbonic gas will rise to the surface and burst, and make rings two or three feet wide …". The so-called Bubbly Creek was so caked with grease and filth that Sinclair observed runaway chickens walking upon the mucky fork. It wasn't until the Union Stock Yards closed in 1971 that Bubbly Creek began ever so slowly to reclaim its once pristine state.

The best way to explore Bubbly Creek is by kayak. From the newly inaugurated Park 571 Boathouse, you can launch a canoe or kayak directly into the northern starting point of the fork and easily paddle its length southward, to the end point at Pershing Road.

Paddling along the Bubbly Creek, it is incredible to see the animals and vegetation that are slowly reclaiming their wetland home. If you are lucky, you might spot mallard ducks navigating the waters, swooping tree swallows, elegant green herons, high-flying hawks or evidence of beavers busily building homes of their own along the banks. But the creek, despite efforts to help speed along the renewal process, still bears witness to its highly polluted past: rebar pokes out from the embankments, plastic bags decorate the trees that flank the creek, and bubbles still rise up from the turbid depths. Though Bubbly Creek still has a long way to go, considering its past, it is truly amazing that one can paddle it and find peace as well as signs of renewal and hope.

Address Park No. 571, 2754 S Eleanor Street, Chicago, IL 60608, +1 (312) 747-6515, www.chicagoparkdistrict.com/parks | **Getting there** Subway to Ashland (Orange Line) | **Tip** Kayak Chicago (+1 (312) 852-9258, kayakchicago.com) offers private, guided kayak tours of Bubbly Creek. If you prefer bringing your own kayak and paddling independently, Park No. 571, the starting point of the South Fork, has a public access launching pier.

18 Bughouse Square

Chicago's premier free speech forum

If you have something to say, pick up your soapbox and head to Bughouse Square. The square is Chicago's most celebrated, improvised, free speech center, located across from the historic Newberry Library in strollworthy Washington Square Park. This orator-friendly square has been hosting poets, religionists, political activists, cranks, and anyone else who has something timely or trivial to get off their chest since the 1920s.

Once a cow path with a well for thirsty cattle, Washington Square Park was transformed during the late 1800s into the bucolic park it is today, with its diagonal walkways bisecting manicured greenery towards a central fountain. In the park's heyday during the Roaring Twenties, revolutionary leftists unofficially began setting up their soapboxes here and declaring their truths. Many of the square's soapbox public speakers became legendary, including radical Lucy Parsons, whom the Chicago Police Department described as "more dangerous than a thousand rioters," anarchist and self-declared hobo doctor Ben Reitman, and Marxist feminist Martha Biegler. The name the square came to be called – Bughouse – is indicative of the public's perception of the early speakers as outrageous, thought to be too far ahead of their times. (The term "bughouse" was slang at the time for a mental health facility.)

In 1964, *Life* magazine profiled the popular square, marking it as a meeting place for gay men and women. In June 1970, Chicago's first Gay Pride March set off proudly from the park towards the Civic Center.

Today a Bughouse Square Committee, headquartered at Newberry Library, still organizes an annual free-speech extravaganza, known as the Bughouse Square Debates, in conjunction with the library's annual book sale.

A memorial tablet at the west end of the park declares Bughouse Square "Chicago's Premier Free Speech Forum."

Address 901 N Clark Street, Chicago, IL 60610, www.chicagoparkdistrict.com/parks | Getting there Subway to Chicago (Red Line) | Tip Free and open to the public, the Newberry Library, located on the northern edge of the square, is home to more than 1.5 million books, 5 million manuscript pages, and 500,000 historic maps. Request to view the 1692 fur trade contract in the museum's collection, which contains one of the earliest references to "Chicagou" (60 W Walton Street, www.newberry.org).

19 Busy Beaver Button Museum

Pin on a button and broadcast your message

The Busy Beaver Button Co. and Button Museum stands as the world's only pin-back button museum. Located within the company's small-scale manufacturing headquarters, this tiny museum displays 9,000 rare, historical buttons. There seems to be a button for every television show, movie, product, and even presidential candidate from past and present (including the "pre-button" made in support of Lincoln's 1864 presidential campaign), a WWII button that depicts Uncle Sam hanging Adolf Hitler from a tree, and an ultra-rare Oswald the Lucky Rabbit button from 1929.

Wearing political buttons, a largely American tradition, began with the inauguration of George Washington in 1789. Supporters of our nation's first president wore "Washington Inaugurals," large, hand-stamped buttons made of copper, brass or Sheffield plate on their coats and breeches. Busy Beaver's "Long Live the President GW" brass button is the oldest and most valuable in the museum's collection.

Busy Beaver Button Co. started in owner Christen Carter's college apartment in the mid-nineties. Four million buttons later, the small company is the leader in the button industry, producing custom buttons made of metal, wood and even 24-karat gold. Every custom button is made with solar power from recycled steel in their geothermally heated/cooled headquarters in the hip Logan Square neighborhood. Busy Beaver's clients include individuals, large corporations, and cultural institutions, from the Brooklyn Brewery to the Art Institute of Chicago. The Busy Beaver Button Museum was unveiled within the production facility in 2010.

As you browse the museum, you can also see button manufacturing in action, as all of the company's buttons are produced onsite, largely by hand. You can even make a button of your very own upon request.

Address 3407 W Armitage Avenue, Chicago, IL 60647, +1 (773) 645-3359, www.busybeaver.net | Getting there Subway to Belmont (Blue Line) and then CTA bus 82 to Kimball & Armitage | Hours Mon–Fri 9am–5:30pm | Tip Discuss pin politics barside at Scofflaw, an elegant corner bar with a Victorian-meets-modern vibe, just a three-minute walk down Armitage Avenue from the Busy Beaver Button Museum. You'll find over 80 types of gin at the antique bar, as well as small plates and a fine selection of American craft beers on draught (3201 W Armitage Avenue, www.scofflawchicago.com).

20_Calumet Fisheries

Seafood shack beside the Blues Brothers' bridge

Who can forget the scene in the iconic 1980 John Landis film, when the Blues Brothers, "Joliet" Jake and Elwood Blues, jump their retired police cruiser over the open 95th Street bascule bridge? Calumet Fisheries, located just off that memorable, moveable bridge on the banks of the heavily industrialized Calumet River in South Deering, saw the scene unfold. This tiny little fish shack has been smoking up sable, salmon, sturgeon, and more marine delights than you can count on ten greasy fingers since the 1920s, long before the Blues Brothers cruised on by.

One of two smokehouses still allowed to burn wood and smoke its fish in the city, this family owned and operated South Side institution smokes all of its seafood on site, stoking the fire and flavor with oak logs, and never, ever using liquid smoke or other industrial substitutes. Before hitting the smoker, the fruits of the seas are marinated overnight. Many customers swear by the golden brown, sweet smoked chubs and salivate over the garlic pepper smoked salmon. Give the smelt – an unofficial Midwestern delicacy – a try too. These finger-sized fish were an invasive species that somehow escaped from Michigan's Crystal Lake into Lake Michigan in the early 1920s.

The smoked goods make up only half of the no-nonsense menu. The other half features fried fish, notably catfish, clam strips, frog's legs, and shrimp. Sides are mostly deep-fat fried, too – think French fries, onion rings, breaded mushrooms, and pickle spears. A side cup of crackers costs just 55 cents.

Don't expect a fancy menu, seating or even bathrooms. This is strictly a take-out business. Do as most diners here do, and dig into your goods right away in the comfort of your car, parked out front. If you're lucky, the drawbridge might pop up – but don't expect another Blues Brothers' style high-jinx jump.

Address 3259 E 95th Street, Chicago, IL 60617, +1 (773) 933-9855, www.calumetfisheries.com | **Getting there** Train to South Chicago (93rd) (Metra Electric Line) | **Hours** Sun–Wed 10am–9:45pm; Thu 9am–9:30pm; Fri & Sat 9am–9:45pm | **Tip** Want to catch and smoke your own fish? River Park, located on the Chicago River at 5100 N Francisco Avenue, near Foster Avenue, is one of the best fishing spots in the city. You'll need an Illinois fishing license, which you can obtain online before you go at www.dnr.illinois.gov.

21 Calumet Water Reclamation Plant

Looking beyond the (toilet) bowl

One hundred and fifty years ago, city sewage dumped into the Chicago River or Lake Michigan, threatening the drinking water and the heath of early Chicagoans. Thanks to the ingenuity of engineers, our city was saved from a swampy, unsanitary fate. On a Calumet Water Retention Plant tour, you can see firsthand how Chicago revolutionized the water treatment arena, as you witness where everyone's poop travels beyond the bowl and what happens to the water that flows down your home's drains.

Organized as the Sanitary District of Chicago in 1889 under an act of the Illinois General Assembly District, the Metropolitan Water Reclamation District is credited with reversing the flow of the Chicago and Calumet River Systems. Today the district continues to protect Lake Michigan, the city's water source, and to guard businesses and homes against flood damage as it manages humanity's vital resource: water.

The District's seven modern water reclamation plants treat residential and industrial wastewater, while also guarding our lakes and rivers against hazardous substances and toxic chemicals. Each day, these hardworking plants clean and recover resources from wastewater as they pump more than 480 million gallons a day of raw sewage.

The plant tour shows you all the action and the magnificent machinery, from the mechanical screens lifting rags and rocks from raw sewage, to the huge circular vats that separate sludge from liquid. You might pick up a few interesting scents along the tour, but this busy plant keeps Chicago safe and healthy while also blazing a new trail in the field of resource recovery. The plant is on the path to become energy neutral by 2023, while also recovering water, biosolids compost, algae for bioplastics, and phosphorus to be sold as fertilizer.

Address 400 E 130th Street, Chicago, IL 60628, +1 (312) 751-6635, www.mwrd.org | Getting there Subway to 95th/Dan Ryan (Red Line) then CTA bus 34 to 130th Street & Daniel Drive | Hours Tours Mon–Fri 9am–1pm. Allow approximately two hours per tour. | Tip You'll need to call +1 (312) 751-6633 or email tours@mwrd.org to reserve your plant tour. Anyone over 18 years of age must provide a scan or photocopy of their state ID or passport for a security check, and present it on the day of tour. For safety, wear long pants and sturdy shoes.

22 Chicago Fire Department Training Facility

Where Mrs. O'Leary's cow kicked over that lantern

"Late one night, when we were all in bed / Mrs. O'Leary lit a lantern in the shed / Her cow kicked it over, then winked her eye and said / 'There'll be a hot time in the old town tonight!'" (Chicago folk song).

Mrs. Catherine O'Leary recalled hearing fiddle music as she got into bed on the night of Sunday, October 8, 1871. Hours later, she awoke to find her small barn at 137 DeKoven Street aflame. Flames whirled across the city. Two days later, more than 2,000 acres of Chicago had burned to the ground, over 300 lives were lost, and 100,000 were left homeless.

The *Chicago Times* jumped to the conclusion that O'Leary had burned down her barn herself. It described the 44-year-old mother of five as "an old Irish woman" who was "bent almost double with the weight of many years of toil, trouble and privation. … The old hag swore she would be revenged on a city that would deny her a bit of wood or a pound of bacon." Theories abound as to who or what caused the Great Chicago Fire, but fingers no longer point towards poor Mrs. O'Leary and her cow. In 1997, Chicago's city council officially exonerated the unlikely duo.

Today the Fire Department's training school stands on the very spot where the fire began. Step inside the lobby to see one of Chicago's original steam-powered engines, as well as a poignant display of the badges and bronzed boots and helmets of firefighters fallen in the line of duty. A 33-foot bronze sculpture of stylized flames entitled *Pillar of Fire* by sculptor Egon Weiner marks where Mrs. O'Leary's cow kicked over the lantern, just outside the academy.

If you smell smoke while visiting the site of Mrs. O'Leary's barn, don't fret: as part of the cadets' training, instructors build live fires.

Address 558 W DeKoven, Chicago, IL 60607, +1 (312) 747-7239, www.cpfta.com | Getting there Subway to Clinton (Blue Line) | Hours Mon–Fri 8:30am–3:30pm | Tip If you want to visit a real-life, former working Chicago firehouse, head to the Fire Museum of Greater Chicago, which is currently housed in what used to be Engine 123's quarters. Photographs, fire-fighting gear and equipment from throughout the ages and even old engines are all on display in this two-story firehouse. Currently the museum is only open on the fourth Saturday of each month, and closed entirely in December (5218 S Western Avenue, www.firemuseumofgreaterchicago.org).

23 The Chicago Harbor Lock

Go with the flow

Once upon a time the Chicago River flowed sluggishly, carrying raw sewage and industrial waste in its slow current directly into the city's water source, Lake Michigan. Typhoid, cholera, and dysentery were rampant, and in 1885, after a heavy rainstorm flushed into the lake beyond the clean water intakes, a whopping 12 percent of the population died of diseases linked to unsafe drinking water.

Determined to provide bustling Chicago with a clean water supply, the newly created Chicago Sanitary District unveiled a system of three canal locks, reversing the Chicago River flow toward the Mississippi River and Gulf of Mexico and diverting sewage away from the clean Lake Michigan water supply. The Chicago Harbor Lock is a working reminder of what is considered one of the most revolutionary civil engineering projects in history, and it remains one of the busiest locks in the nation.

Operated by the U.S. Army Corps of Engineers, this lock is one of two gateways from the Great Lakes to the Chicago Area Waterway System. It takes a mesmerizing 12 to 15 minutes to cycle through a typical water-level difference of two to five feet, using the power of gravity to control water levels through partially opened Chicago Harbor Lock gates. Its chamber can hold up to 100 vessels at once, with over 40,000 passing through each year. It is a marvel to watch as the lock light turns green and kayaks, canoes, pontoons, water taxis, luxury yachts, and sailboats make the mad dash from Lake Michigan into the lock. Once inside, the water level lowers, a horn sounds, and it's another race into the reversed Chicago River.

Thanks to the Chicago Harbor Lock and other river cleanup efforts, the Chicago River is much cleaner today. Though it's no longer called "the stinking river," a sign posted near the lock sums up its current state: "The Chicago River has a lot of charm, but don't fall in!"

Address The Chicago Harbor Lock is located on the Chicago River, south of Navy Pier, and is accessible by marine vessel. You can also view the lock in action from the bike-friendly Lakefront Trail at North Streeter Drive. | **Tip** Board a Wendella Signature Lake and River Tour, and you'll voyage down the Chicago River, cruise into the Chicago Harbor Lock, and sail along the shores of Lake Michigan (+1 (312) 337-1446, www.wendellaboats.com).

24_Chicago Honey Co-op

Saving the honeybees, one hive at a time

If you spot a swarm of honeybees while you are strolling the streets of Chicago, you are not dreaming. The city is absolutely abuzz with bees thanks to Chicago Honey Co-op, a Lawndale-based organization that combines job training with the art of beekeeping. Since 2004, more than fifty beehives have buzzed with bees at their three urban apiaries. These city-dwelling bees buzz around Humboldt, Garfield, and Douglas Parks, where a variety of flower and tree species coupled with diverse, highly concentrated nectars, make for an intensely flavored, all-natural, delicious honey. In addition to producing and selling raw honey, this sweet co-op teaches beekeeping, trains with hard-to-employ Chicagoans, and advocates sustainable agriculture.

If you want to see the Chicago Honey Co-op's bees in action, head to one of their three bee farms. Schulze & Burch Biscuit Company (1133 W 35th Street) in Bridgeport is home to about 20 hives, and the green rooftop of Christy Webber Landscaping (2900 W Ferdinand Street) hosts a handful of hives. Twelve hives are located in Back of the Yards near 51st and Racine, and two hives call Patchwork Farms (2825 W Chicago Avenue) home. If you're lucky, you might see beekeepers at work dressed in their light-hued suits and netted hats, checking each hive's "super"– vertical drawers where the bees store their honey. Puffs from the odd, teapot-shaped smoke machine help to calm the buzzing bees, while a large brush is used gently to brush the bees away from the supers, revealing the sweet, sticky treasure.

Chicago Honey Co-op is a community resource that produces more than just amber waves of certified natural honey. As the number of native bees is seeing sharp declines, this co-op passes the beekeeping torch to budding urban apiculturists while also fostering the community and saving the honeybees, one hive at a time.

Address 2000 W Carroll Avenue, Chicago, IL 60612, +1 (312) 508-8142, www.chicagohoneycoop.com | **Getting there** Subway to Ashland (Green and Pink Line) | **Hours** Apiary hours vary according to season and weather conditions; call ahead to confirm. | **Tip** If you'd rather avoid the bees, you can also purchase Chicago Co-op Honey from the hive-free Green City Market, Chicago's only year-round, sustainable farmers' market. Located on the south end of Lincoln Park (1817 N Clark Street, www.greencitymarket.com) from May through October, this glorious, green market moves into the Peggy Notebaert Nature Museum (2430 N Cannon Drive, www.naturemuseum.org) from November through April.

25 Chicago Motor Club Inn

Trippy monument to motorism

The grand Chicago Motor Club building is Chicago's finest Art Deco-style skyscraper. When it formally opened on January 28, 1929, a Chicago Tribune reporter referred to it as "a monument to the progress of motordom." Originally designed by Chicago architectural firm Holabird and Root, in 2004 this 15-story skyscraper stood unoccupied and in danger of falling into complete disrepair. Thankfully, Hampton Inn stepped in, completely renovating the building and transforming it into a fabulous hotel that honors Chicago's original temple of transportation.

Founded by a group of automobile enthusiasts who shared an interest in both auto touring and racing, the Chicago Motor Club, which eventually merged into AAA, embraced road travel by providing maps, travel itineraries and hotel guides. The club offered visitors the chance to plan their new big trip thanks to TripTiks, maps that also provided tips on where to eat and stay along the highway, available in the lobby.

A 30-by-20-foot road map mural, painted by Chicago artist John Warner Norton, and still located above the elevators in the grand, two-story lobby, provided inspiration. Motor Club visitors studied the mural while dreaming up travel plans by following the grey lines, or the 19 national highways that existed in 1928, from Chicago to their desired, fantasy destination. An original, 1928 Ford Model A – the first Ford to use a standard set of driver controls including clutch and brake pedals, throttle, and gearshift – overlooks the lobby from the mezzanine.

"From the moment guests walk into the lobby, one immediately knows that this building is special," enthuses Ross Guthrie, the hotel's general manager. "The large mural of the map is stunning. We love telling the story of the building and sharing the integral part of history this building has had in Chicago and AAA."

Address 68 E Wacker Place, Chicago, IL 60601, +1 (312) 419-9014, www.hamptoninn3.hilton.com | Getting there Subway to State / Lake (Brown, Orange, Purple, Green, and Pink Line) | Tip Try the "Giggle Water" (the code name for booze during Prohibition), a cocktail complete with gin, rum, tonic, simple syrup, lime, and parsley, with a splash of bourbon, at Jack's Place, the lobby bar.

26 Chicago Pizza & Oven Grinder Co.

Deep-dish pizza with a side of mob history

At 10:30am on February 14, 1929, four men packing two Thompson submachine guns burst into a garage at 2122 N Clark Street. They shot dead seven men of the North Side Irish gang associated with the Irish gangster George "Bugs" Moran, one of Al Capone's long-time enemies. Though the Saint Valentine's Day Massacre, as it came to be called, was never officially linked to Capone, most hold him responsible for the murders. And though the garage was demolished in 1967, you can still dig into a unique deep-dish pizza at the three-story brownstone building that likely served as a lookout, located just across the street.

Chicago Pizza & Oven Grinder Co. is best known for a one-of-a-kind take on Chicago-style deep-dish pizza that many refer to as an upside-down pizza in a bowl. "Made from scratch" with triple-raised Sicilian bread-type dough; a tangy homemade sauce brewed to perfection with olive oil, fresh garlic, onions, green peppers, whole plum tomatoes and a special blend of cheeses; sausage made from prime Boston butts; and whole, fresh mushrooms – pizzas here arrive tableside for eager diners to bite into. Oven Grinder Co. pizzas fall more within the pot pie classification: large, deep, and stuffed to the brim. They are baked in a crock, their dough puffed up several inches above the edge.

Rumor has it that the garage served as a lookout post for Capone's henchmen. Some 70 rounds of ammunition were fired on that fateful Valentine's Day, which many say marked the beginning of Capone's downfall. No one was brought to trial for the murders. Capone was subpoenaed, posted bond, and was released, only to be arrested in Philadelphia on charges of carrying concealed weapons. He served a mere nine months in prison before being released for good behavior.

Address 2121 N Clark Street, Chicago, IL 60614, +1 (773) 248-2570, www.chicagopizzaandovengrinder.com | Getting there Subway to Sedgwick (Brown and Purple Line) | Hours Mon–Thu 4pm–11pm; Fri 4pm–midnight; Sat 11:30am–midnight; Sun 11:30am–11pm | Tip The Chicago History Museum's incredible virtual reality app *Chicago 00: The St. Valentine's Day Massacre* offers a YouTube video and Google Street View experience, with images of the site of the massacre that can be viewed as high-resolution, 360° panoramas. Both experiences can be accessed online at www.chicago00.org.

27 Chicago Underground Comedy

Sanctuary for the uncommon comedian

In a punk-rock setting on an infamous Tuesday nighttime slot, Chicago's hilarious comedians hit the stage of Lakeview's Beat Kitchen for Chicago Underground Comedy, or ChUC as it is best known, the second longest running and the most out-of-the box and under-the-radar comedy show in the city. Committed to weirdness, the lineups at this intimate show always include a sketch, character, and variety act, interspersing stand up with something spicy and different to cleanse the palette, as well as an act you couldn't even begin to classify.

With tickets running at a whopping $5, ChUC stands as a laughably cheap date night. A percentage of ticket proceeds are dedicated to ChUC Charities, the show's in-house fundraising effort, which raises money for community-focused charities, giving you an even bigger bang for your buck.

Since 2005, ChUC has launched some of the most clever, innovative minds in the business, while also providing a sanctuary for comedians who just want to have fun and connect, and not necessarily do their tightest (or cleanest) ten minutes for the audience. Everyone has graced the small stage, from T. J. Miller to Cameron Esposito, Kyle Kinane to Hannibal Buress, Beth Stelling to Kumail Nanjiani.

As an alt-comedy haven, ChUC revels in its reputation as a comics' playground. Silly goofs, wacky antics, and plain old tomfoolery are always welcome. This playground is also committed to inclusivity: women, people of color, and the LGBT community are reflected in the especially diverse lineups. Plan on trading a few laughs for tears, too, as the last Tuesday of the month is dedicated to Comedy Secrets, a secrets-and-sadness storytelling based show.

The show starts at 9:30pm every Tuesday night at the Beat Kitchen and usually rocks a full house, so arrive early to save your seats.

Address Beat Kitchen, 2100 W Belmont Avenue, Chicago, IL 60618, www.chicagoundergroundcomedy.com | Getting there Subway to Belmont (Red and Blue Line) then CTA bus 77 to Belmont & Hoyne | Hours Tue 9:30pm, doors open 9pm | Tip Beat Kitchen serves up hearty pub grub during ChUC. Build your own pizza or dig into the spicy mac 'n' cheese while you enjoy the show. Save room for a homemade brownie (www.beatkitchen.com).

28 Chris's Billiards

The color of money

Chris's Billiards boasts, "It's not what's new, it's what's not new that's great." Not much has changed since legendary director Martin Scorsese stepped in this Portage Park gem and declared it the backdrop for the timeless pool-hall tale *The Color of Money*.

When production manager Dodie Foster arrived in Canada, where the movie was originally set to be filmed, he was disappointed to find mostly snooker tables. So he brought Scorsese to his hometown of Chicago and ushered him up the long staircase that leads to Chris's second-floor hall. The dozens of framed photographs of championship players on the walls made it obvious that this was a pool hall for professionals, and Scorsese cast Chris's as the hall where pool shark Fast Eddie Felson (played by Paul Newman in the movie) would groom Vincent Lauria (a young Tom Cruise) for pool stardom.

Chris's remains a place for players who are looking for low rates and good competition, making it an excellent place to learn the ropes of the game. Forty tables – ten seven-foot pool tables, twenty-nine nine-foot pool tables, and one twelve-foot snooker table – clack with both amateurs and pros. When you are not playing, settle into the bleachers and watch the tournaments go down. The competitions, with cash payouts of up to $5,000, have drawn the best pool players from around the world, including 1994 world champion Sang Lee, making Chris's a place where you can both learn and play beside or against the pros. As an added bonus, it is BYOB.

A musty smell lingers in the air, and pool sharks search high and low for their next meal ticket. The felt on the tables is worn. The stucco walls have taken in a lot of cigarette smoke over the years. But these are the telltale signs that Chris's is the real deal, with tables that play fast and zero room for restraint when it comes to the English you put on the cue ball.

Address 4637 N Milwaukee Avenue, Chicago, IL 60630, +1 (773) 286-4714, www.chrissbilliards.com | Getting there Subway to Jefferson Park (Blue Line) | Hours Daily 9–2am | Tip Coffee shop by day and bar at night, Surge Coffee Bar & Billiards boasts 14 Brunswick Crown V pool tables and a modern, smoke-free, and friendly ambiance (3241 W Montrose Avenue, +1 (773) 961-8096, surgebilliards.com).

29_Cindy's Rooftop

Where every hour is the happiest hour

If you are looking for Chicago's most beautiful people, you will find them on the terrace of Cindy's Rooftop, the shining, steel-framed crown jewel perched atop the Chicago Athletic Association Hotel. Thanks to the sweeping, Instagram-worthy views of Millennium Park, Michigan Avenue, and Lake Michigan beyond, this open-air terrace with its accompanying glass sunroof-topped restaurant is a – if not *the* – place to see and be seen, especially in the summertime, when the beach-house vibe and streaming sunlight beckon Chicago's brightest and most winsome citizens, suited and sun-dressed for some breezy happy-hour mingling.

Cindy's Rooftop caps the elegant Venetian Gothic building – designed by Henry Ives Cobb and completed in 1893 – that once housed the elite Chicago Athletic Association. Marshall Field, Cyrus McCormick, and William Wrigley used to play sports and party here. In 2007, the 122-year-old, 11-story building was totally restored and transformed into a luxe, 241-room hotel. Fittingly, the rooftop of what was once a men's only club was named in honor of Chicago philanthropist extraordinaire Cindy Pritzker.

The main dining room is delightfully romantic, with its long cherry-wood picnic-style tables and benches, designed to encourage conversation while dining on seasonal, shared plates and handcrafted cocktails under the warm glow of string lights hanging from the glass rooftop. But if you are in the mood for a love affair with Chicago, make a beeline for the outside terrace, which you will find drenched in sunshine on sizzling summer days, buzzing under a moonlit sky at night, and kept cozy by fireplaces in the cooler months. Try to visit on a Wednesday or Saturday evening, in the summertime, when fireworks launched from Navy Pier light up the sky above. The spectacular view will quite simply take your breath away any time.

Address 12 S Michigan Avenue, Chicago, IL 60603, +1 (312) 792-3502, www.cindysrooftop.com | Getting there Subway to Monroe (Red Line) | Hours Mon–Fri 11–1am; Sat 10–2am; Sun 10am–midnight | Tip Catch Navy Pier's fireworks spectacular from Cindy's Rooftop when they launch on Wednesdays at 9:30pm and Saturdays at 10pm throughout the summer, from Memorial Day through Labor Day.

30__Civil War Memorial at St. James Cathedral

Faith over fire

At 9pm on October 8, 1871, a fire started in a small barn just southwest of Chicago's Loop. When flaming debris blew across the river, advancing the fire towards the ritzy Near North neighborhood of McCormickville, panic set in. The bells of St. James Cathedral rang close to midnight, warning the wealthy residents that their lives were in danger. More than 2,000 city acres had been flattened; 100,000 of Chicago's 300,000 inhabitants were left homeless. Only the stone walls, bell tower, and Civil War Memorial of St. James Cathedral, the oldest Episcopal Church in Chicago and a cornerstone of the neighborhood, had survived the fire.

When early settler Juliette Kinzie founded the parish here in 1834 by, this plot of land was surrounded by a vast wilderness. The city of Chicago was still but a dream. As the smoke began to clear that fateful fall, the weary yet faithful neighborhood parishioners built a temporary chapel on the site as soon as rubble had been cleared away. They gathered before the Civil War Memorial, which served as a makeshift altar, and held their first, poignant, post-fire mass.

The elaborate, mid-Victorian Civil War memorial was dedicated to parishioners who served during the bloodiest war in U.S. history. Located today in the cathedral's narthex, the memorial features the names of seventy members who had enlisted in the Union Army; ten lost their lives. President elect Abraham Lincoln attended services at St. James on November 25, 1860. A plaque set in the north wall of the narthex honors his role in the Civil War.

Four years after the fire, on October 9, 1875, services were held in the rebuilt cathedral. At the top of the surviving bell tower, note the black stones, soot-stained from the Chicago Fire, a powerful reminder of the worst disaster in Chicago's history.

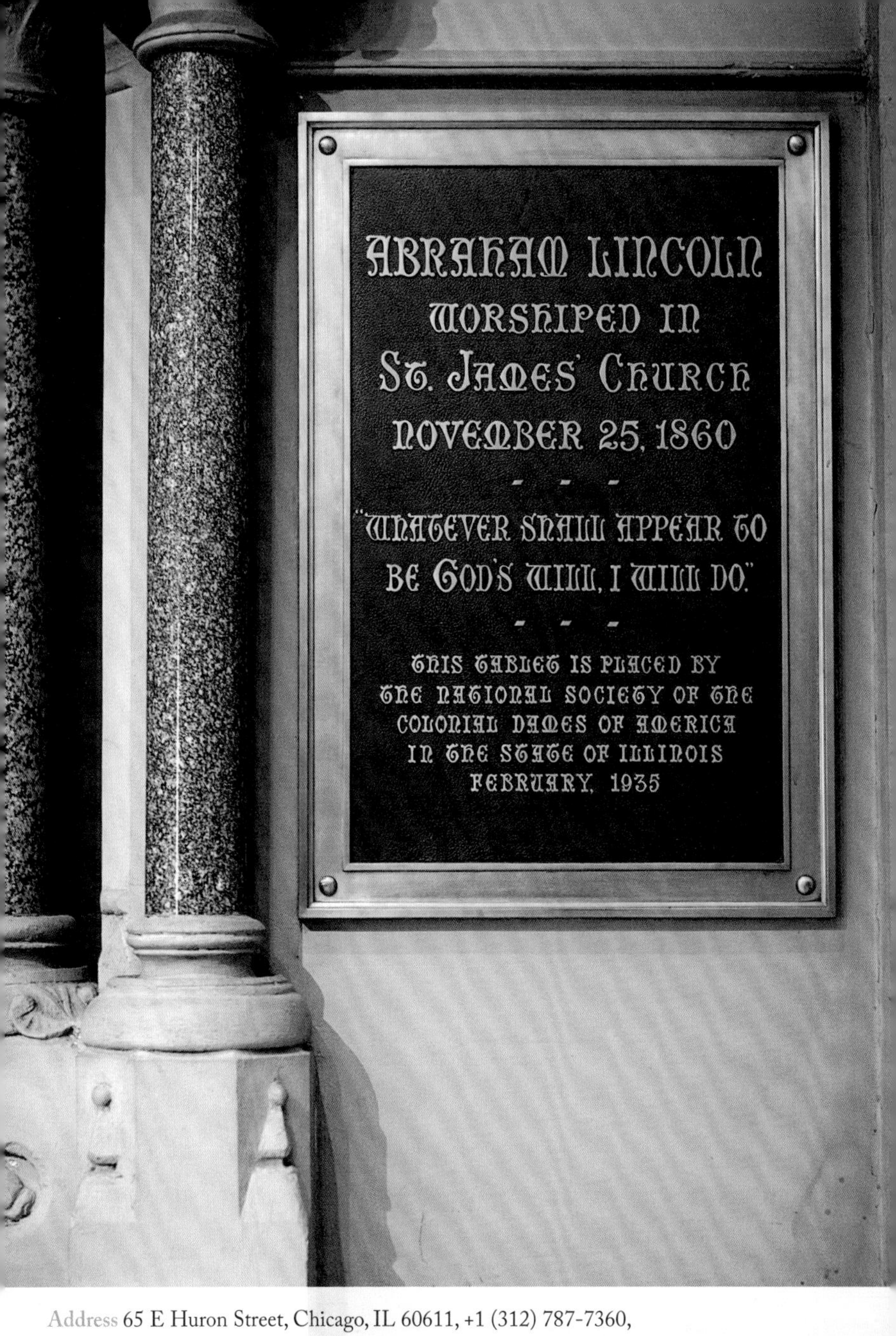

Address 65 E Huron Street, Chicago, IL 60611, +1 (312) 787-7360, www.saintjamescathedral.org | Getting there Subway to Chicago (Red Line) | Hours Mon–Fri 8:30am–5:30pm; Sun 8am–2pm | Tip Take a moment to find inner peace by walking the cathedral's hidden outdoor labyrinth, located in the oasis-like plaza adjacent to St. James, at the corner of Huron and Rush Streets.

31_Clarke House

Portrait of pre-Civil War Chicago

The Clarke House is a true survivor – 188 years and counting. She took the heat of several fires, saw cholera kill within her walls, was ripped from her foundation, was forced to jump the L tracks, and was moved not once but twice to a different location. She saw her owner fall into financial ruin. Some of her elegant rooms were used to butcher livestock. She even found herself suspended in mid-air for two weeks, when the hydraulic equipment used to relocate the home froze during the frigid winter of 1977.

Owner Henry B. Clarke, a New Yorker by birth who relocated to Chicago in 1835 and made his mark selling guns, boots, and leather, was one of the first wealthy settlers to build south of the river. In 1836, the homestead where he would raise his six children with his wife Caroline, rose from the prairie on 20-plus acres of land near the intersection of today's Michigan Avenue and 16th/17th Streets. The Greek Revival Clarke House with its Doric columns and porticos reflected the period's obsession with ancient civilization.

When the Panic of 1837 hit, a bankrupt Clarke farmed and hunted for wild game in the surrounding prairie, and used the south parlors for meat processing and storage. In 1849, Henry died of cholera. His young widow sold 17 acres of the surrounding land and added the Italianate belvedere, her own unforgettable touch.

After Caroline's death, the home experienced two high-jinx moves, first to 4536 South Wabash Avenue, and finally, on a bitter cold December night, to its present location just a few blocks from its original location. Today the home offers a glimpse into the life of a middle-class family in pre-Civil War era Chicago, thanks to its carefully curated contents. It's easy to imagine the Clarke family gathered by the hearthstone in the Northeast Sitting Room, singing songs together beside the fortepiano or strolling through their garden.

Address 1827 S Indiana Avenue, Chicago, IL 60616, +1 (312) 744-3316, www.cityofchicago.org | **Getting there** Subway to Cermak-Chinatown (Red Line) | **Hours** Tours on Wed, Fri & Sat 1pm and 2:30pm | **Tip** Adjacent to the Clarke House, the Chicago Women's Park and Gardens (1801 S Indiana Avenue, Chicago, IL 60616, www.chicagoparkdistrict.com/parks/chicago-womens-park-and-gardens) honor the contributions women have made to the City of Chicago throughout its history. A series of carved granite hands atop granite bases, a work known as "Helping Hands" by Louise Bourgeois, pays homage to pioneer social reformer Jane Addams (1860–1935).

32 Colleen Moore Fairy Castle

All that glitters is gold and miniature

Colleen Moore envisioned the ultimate enchanted fairy castle, filled with sumptuous, antique furnishings, dripping with diamond accents, alight with golden chandeliers, and resplendent in royal regalia. In its kitchen, the copper stove that once threatened to burn Hansel and Gretel alive now bakes a four-and-twenty-blackbird pie. King Arthur's round table, set with solid gold plates and cutlery, awaits its brave guests at the center of the tapestry-lined dining hall. Sleeping Beauty once slept in the master bedroom, her bedspread made of golden spiderwebs. In the library over 80 books, including the world's tiniest bible, wait patiently to be read. At the entrance, a magical coach waits to take a princess to a ball. It cost a staggering $500,000 to build this dreamy castle, the equivalent of $7 million in today's money. But don't plan on moving in just yet: this magnificent castle measures just nine square feet.

Colleen Moore was an early Hollywood silent-film star with a passion for miniatures. In 1928, she hired famed Hollywood architect and set designer Horace Jackson to create the floor plan and layout for her dream dollhouse, and hired art director and designer Harold Grieve, who had revamped Colleen Moore's personal, Bel Air mansion, to create elaborate interiors. Moore, not only an actress but also a savvy businesswoman, organized a national tour for the dollhouse to raise money for children's charities. The delightful dollhouse made its way across the US in toy departments of stores in major cities.

In 1949, the Fairy Castle made its final stop at the Museum of Science and Industry, where it now rests in a lower-level corner. See if you can spot the tiny cradle that sits on the rocking tree in the Magic Garden. Made with jewelry from her grandmother, this cradle was Colleen Moore's most cherished miniature *objet d'art*.

Address Museum of Science and Industry, Lower Level, 5700 S Lake Shore Drive, Chicago, IL 60637, +1 (773) 684-1414, www.msichicago.org | Getting there Train to 55th-56th-57th Street (Metra Electric and South Shore Line) | Hours Daily 9:30am–4pm; check website for extended hours and exceptions | Tip If Tom Thumb were to plan a Chicago move, he could take his pick between Colleen Moore's luxe Fairy Castle and the 68 Thorne Miniature Rooms at the Art Institute of Chicago. Conceived by Mrs. James Ward Thorne of Chicago and built between 1932 and 1940, these tiny rooms, constructed on a scale of one inch to one foot, showcase rich interiors ranging from the late 13th century to the 1930s (111 S Michigan Avenue).

33 Confederate Mound

Mass grave of Civil War prisoners

The largest mass grave in the western hemisphere, containing the remains of thousands of Confederate prisoners of war killed at Camp Douglas, is hidden in a quiet corner of the Great Grand Crossing neighborhood. The Confederate Mound Memorial, located in the southwest section of Oak Woods Cemetery, is the only recognition of the service, suffering, and death of the approximately 6,000 men who are buried beneath the 30-foot granite column.

From January 1863 until the end of the war in May 1865, Camp Douglas, which stood at the edge of the prairie on Chicago's South Side, served as a Union Army organizational and training camp for volunteer regiments and ultimately a detention camp for paroled Confederate prisoners pending their formal exchange for Union prisoners. With a death rate averaging 20 percent, it is estimated that more than 6,000 Confederate prisoners died in detention here from disease, starvation, and the bitter cold winters from 1862 through 1865. The bodies of the dead were originally buried at the City Cemetery near Lake Michigan in Lincoln Park, which was then abandoned. From 1865 to 1867, they were exhumed and re-interred in this mass grave, known as Confederate Mound.

Confederate Mound is an oval-shaped plot, located between Divisions 1 and 2 of Section K in the park-like cemetery. Capping the column is a bronze statue of a Confederate soldier, based on the painting *Appomattox* by John A. Elder. The bas-relief images at the base include *A Soldier's Death Dream*, which depicts a fallen soldier and his horse on the battlefield. The monument was designed by General John C. Underwood and dedicated on May 30, 1895 by President Grover Cleveland before an estimated 100,000 onlookers. Four cannons surround the monument, with 12 marble headstones placed between it and the northern cannon, to mark the graves of unknown Camp Douglas Union guards.

Address 1035 E 67th Street, Chicago, IL 60637, +1 (773) 288-3800 | Getting there Train to Stoney Island (Metra Electric Line) | Hours Daily 8am–4:30pm | Tip While you're at Oak Woods Cemetery, pay your respects to other notable residents, including Chicago Mayor Harold Washington, crime boss Giacomo "Big Jim" Colosimo, Olympian Jesse Owens, civil rights activist Ida B. Wells, and physicist Enrico Fermi.

34 Couch Mausoleum

A stately reminder of a graveyard past

Strolling through lovely Lincoln Park with its flowers, verdant fields, ponds, and pathways, it is hard to believe that there are thousands of people buried beneath your feet.

Yet the southern edge of this lakefront park did indeed serve as the city cemetery. During the 19th century, Chicago buried its dead at the many religious graveyards and family-owned gravesites here, while the Potter's Field, located where the park's baseball diamond is today, welcomed indigent souls. It wasn't until 1864, after a doctor declared that it was unsafe to bury the dead so close to the lake, where bodily fluids and bacteria could so easily ooze out from the graves below to the water table, that city officials decided to relocate the bodies and turn this tranquil tract of land into a park. Workers transferred many of the deceased to other city cemeteries, but it was far too costly and difficult to remove the Couch Mausoleum, with its heavy stones fastened tightly together with copper rivets.

Ira Couch arrived in Chicago from New York in 1836. A tailor by trade, wise land and real estate acquisitions made him an early Chicago millionaire. He died in 1857, while wintering in Cuba, and his body was shipped back to Chicago, where he was entombed in this iron-fenced mausoleum, only his last name carved in stone over the vault's entrance. Other family members were likely later interred in this the family tomb, but no one knows exactly who rests eternally beside Ira.

In 1998, workers digging the site for the adjacent Chicago History Museum's parking garage in Lincoln Park (1731 N Clark Street) discovered the remains of more than 80 people, including one perfectly preserved in a sealed, 19th-century iron coffin. Ira Couch may or may not rest alone in his iron-gated tomb, but certainly many of his unmoved contemporaries still lie buried near him in the surrounding park.

Address Southwest corner of Lincoln Park, near N Clark Street and W LaSalle Drive, Chicago, IL | Getting there Subway to Sedgwick (Brown and Purple Line) | Tip A boulder of Wisconsin granite marks the grave of David Kennison, the only other visible clue to Lincoln Park's graveyard past, near N Clark Street and Wisconsin Street. Though many doubt Kennison's outrageous claims, he declared himself the last survivor of the Boston Tea Party, a scout for George Washington, a survivor of both the Battle of Bunker Hill and the massacre at Fort Dearborn – and the Daughters of the American Revolution stand by him. A plaque on the boulder states that he died at the whopping age of 115 years, 3 months and 17 days.

35 Doane Observatory

Spy on galaxies far, far away

If you've ever dreamed of spying on the farthest galaxies in the universe – even trillions of miles away – the Doane Observatory, almost hidden on the shores of Lake Michigan just east of the Adler Planetarium's main building, promises to show you distant, celestial objects. Built in 1977, the observatory houses one of the nation's few astronomical telescopes located in a major city. The Doane's classical, 500-plus-pound Cassegrain reflector, together with its 20-inch-diameter mirror, gather over 5,000 times more light than an unaided human eye, allowing for long focal lengths and potentially high magnifications despite its relatively short telescope tube.

The Doane is constantly in motion – at the same rate as the earth rotates – from atop its banana-yellow, fork-style equatorial mounting. This movement keeps celestial objects centered in the field of view at all times so they can be watched for extended periods of time, although special limit switches prevent it from rotating in a full circle. If you've ever wanted to spot sunspots, the Doane also houses a Coronado SolarMax 90 hydrogen-alpha telescope and a dense filter for the "white-light" telescope, so you can stare directly into the sun.

Climb the small spiral staircase into the dome that houses the telescope, then climb another metal staircase, peer into the aperture and prepare to be amazed. Despite the bright city lights, the views to the east over Lake Michigan are strikingly clear.

The Doane Observatory is open for daytime telescope views of the sun from 10am to 1pm every day, weather permitting. Inquire at the box office when you arrive at the Adler Planetarium or call ahead to see if it will be open the day of your planned visit. Note that since use of the observatory is highly dependent on weather conditions and volunteer schedules, the daily schedule may change at a moment's notice.

Address 1300 S Lake Shore Drive, Chicago, IL 60605, +1 (312) 922-7827, www.adlerplanetarium.org | Getting there Subway to Roosevelt (Red, Orange, and Green Line), connect to CTA bus 146 at State and Roosevelt Road. | Hours Daily 10am–1pm, although hours vary due to weather conditions, so call ahead | Tip Don't miss the opportunity to step into Adler Planetarium's historic Atwood Sphere, Chicago's oldest large-scale mechanical planetarium, constructed in 1913. Step into the slowly rotating, 17-feet-diameter sphere and watch as the brightest stars of the night sky appear via the 692 holes in its metal surface. Pilots once learned to navigate the nighttime sky from the comfort of this sphere.

36__Doughnut Vault

Get 'em while they're hot

Stroll down Franklin Street in River North early on any given morning, in rain, snow, sleet, or sunshine, and you'll see a line snaking out the door of a tiny shop. No matter the wait, no matter the weather, Chicagoans will do anything to get their hands on the goods held in this one-of-a-kind vault. The sweet smell of fresh, pillowy doughnuts and hot roasted coffee draws Chicagoans to the Doughnut Vault like bees to honey.

In spring 2011, Doughnut Vault ushered in the doughnut craze with its artisanal take on traditional favorites and imaginative new flavors. Three doughnuts are always on the menu, painted on the brick building outside the door: the very dunkable buttermilk old fashioned, the light-as-air gingerbread, and the plain glazed, available in chestnut, vanilla, and chocolate. You will also find one or two extra surprise, seasonally-inspired flavors. Think strawberry-cherry old fashioneds in the summertime, pumpkin cake and apple cider crumble in the autumn. Chestnut cream and mocha hazelnut crunch doughnuts warm bellies on cold winter days, while lemon poppyseeds are a spring delight. The doughnuts here – which purport to be the best in the city, if not in the United States, are fried fresh in small batches to preserve quality. Don't forget to grab a cup of specialty Metropolis blend roasted coffee, the perfect doughnut dunking accompaniment.

An antique brass cash register rings up orders the old-fashioned way, moving the line steadily along. There is nowhere to sit down inside this 5-by-10-foot space fashioned of brick and reclaimed wood; however, outside, a communal table awaits those who must indulge rather than wait till they get home. By all accounts, you must arrive early because once they run out of the daily batch of doughy delights, the shop closes up for the day, sometimes as early as an hour after opening their exclusive vault of sweets.

Address 401 N Franklin Street, Chicago, IL 60654, +1 (312) 285-2830, www.doughnutvault.com | Getting there Subway to Merchandise Mart (Brown and Purple Line) | Hours Mon–Fri 8am until sold out; Sat & Sun 9:30am until sold out | Tip Visit Doughnut Vault on Twitter @doughnutvault to check out the daily menu as well as location updates of the Vault Van, a retro food truck that travels the city peddling everybody's favorite doughnuts and coffee.

37 Dovetail Brewery

The magic behind the beer

Hidden on a corner of Belle Plaine Avenue, wild Chicago-born yeast blows in through the third-floor window of the Dovetail Brewery, magically turning water into some of the best Lambic-style beers in Chicago. This microbrewery's sublime German-style Lager, Bavarian-style Hefeweizen, Franconian-style Rauchbier, and Vienna-style Lager are brewed with the same traditional methods that produce the kind of beers found in small, family-run breweries in Europe. The water is filtered and formulated for each beer; the malt sourced from specialty maltsters in Franconia; and the raw wheat drawn directly from farmers within 150 miles of Chicago.

Co-founders Hagen Dost and Bill Wesselink, both from Chicago, met at beer school in Munich. They returned to Chicago with a plan: to produce beer of the highest quality, similar to the level of craftsmanship found in fine, old-school woodworking. They named their beloved brewery Dovetail, after the dovetail joint, a classic symbol of quality and craftsmanship.

See how beer bubbles to life with a brewery tour, held every Saturday beginning at 11am. You'll taste the malt, feel the hops run through your fingers, see everything from a 120-plus-year-old copper mash from the 1000-year-old Weihenstephan pilot brewery in Germany, to a magnificent, custom-built *koelschip*, and sample three beers as you wander through the 22,000-square-foot facility. If you're lucky, a proud Dost will be your guide.

Outside of the brewery, you'll be hard-pressed to find the highly sought-after small batch brews. Dovetail self-distributes its beer in kegs, focusing on major beer venues in Chicago and other locations in the immediate vicinity within two miles of the brewery. The in-brewery Tap Room is family- and dog-friendly and guests are welcome to bring their own food (BYOF), making it the perfect spot to sip a flight of Dovetail's flagship brews.

Address 1900 W Belle Plaine Avenue, Chicago, IL 60613, +1 (773) 683-1414, www.dovetailbrewery.com | Getting there Subway to Irving Park (Brown Line) | Hours Tours, Sat 11am; Tap Room, Tue–Thu 2–10pm; Fri noon–11pm; Sat 11am–11pm; Sun 10am–8pm | Tip Food trucks roll up curbside to Dovetail Brewery on a weekly basis, making it easier than ever to pair beer with your fave food truck delights. Check the event page at www. dovetailbrewery.com/events for upcoming food truck visits and more.

38__Fantasy Costumes

Reveal your true identity

Are you in urgent need of a gorilla suit? A latex mask of (jailed) former governor Rod Blagojevich? A Cheshire cat headpiece? An adhesive handlebar mustache? A George Washington-style colonial era wig? Fishnet stockings that fit a 350-pound person? Fantasy Costumes has you covered. This amazing, oversized shop, located in the historic Six Corners shopping district, offers an entire city block packed with over one million fanciful outfits as well as wigs, masks and makeup for every season and creative reason.

What started out as a small wigs-only store morphed into one of the biggest costume shops in the world as owner George Garcia gradually took over neighboring storefronts on this stretch of Milwaukee Avenue, and gathered an inventory that promises to costume customers from head to toe. More of a costume mall than a shop, Fantasy Costume's 18,000 square feet of floor space guarantee you'll find everything you need to become any character or beast.

With thousands of new items added each year, it's easy to get lost among the merchandise, which fills every corner, nook, cranny, and crevice from floor to ceiling. October during Halloween season, which accounts for about 40 percent of annual sales, it can be especially difficult to make your way around the many crowded rooms, each dedicated to a costume element. But the creative team members here, who are also known to hide behind boxes and pop out to scare customers, will point you in the right direction. In the two weeks leading up to the scariest day of the year, Fantasy Costumes is conveniently open 24 hours a day.

This is a place where anyone can find the tools and tricks they need to embrace even their most outlandish fantasies. Fantasy Costumes' mission hasn't changed over the last five decades: "We strive to help customers look great while having fun. And it's OK to get a little crazy."

Address 4065 N Milwaukee Avenue, Chicago, IL 60641, +1 (773) 777-0222, www.fantasycostumes.com | Getting there Subway to Montrose (Blue Line) | Hours Mon–Sat 9:30am–8pm; Sun 11am–5pm | Tip Also located at Six Corners, the 1,938-seat Portage Theater stands as one of the oldest movie houses in Chicago. Its annual organist-accompanied Silent Film Festival, hosted every August, is not to be missed (4050 N Milwaukee Avenue, www.theportagetheater.com).

39_Fern House

The Midwest as it was 300 million years ago

If you're looking to escape the brutal Chicago winter, fly away to the Garfield Park Conservatory, the perfect tropical vacation spot within the city during the winter months. At 4.5 acres, this botanical treasure is one of the largest greenhouse conservatories in the United States. Its lush, verdant Fern House offers not only a warm, welcome respite from the polar vortex, but also a glimpse of what the Midwest might have looked like millions of years ago.

Located in the midst of historic Garfield Park on Chicago's West Side, the conservatory was designed by renowned Prairie-style landscape architect Jens Jensen, and opened to the public in 1907. Jensen's goal of recreating naturalistic landscapes under the glass top, a revolutionary idea at the time, is nowhere more evident than in the Fern House, where primitive plants – plants that grew during the age of the dinosaurs, about 300 million years ago – rest on rocky outcroppings and surround a koi-filled lagoon.

Wandering among the cycads, which are ancient cone-bearing plants, ferns, mosses and liverworts, one would expect an acrotholus to pop out at any minute. Cycads can live up to 500 years, and some of the ones in this room are estimated to be over 300 years old. There are few flowers in the Fern House, since ferns don't have seeds or flowers: gently lift the fern's fronds and look at their undersides to see if you can spot the spores, single cell organisms that grow on these undersides, forming a wide variety of intricate patterns. Dispersed by wind, when a spore lands in the right environment, a new fern is born.

The waterfall at the back of this room is a reminder of Jens Jensen's unique, perfectionist vision for this particular house of the conservatory: he forced his mason to build and rebuild the bubbling waterfall several times until the falling water trickled to the beat of Mendelssohn's *Spring Song*.

Address Garfield Park Conservatory, 300 N Central Park Avenue, Chicago, IL 60624, +1 (312) 746-5100, www.garfieldconservatory.org | Getting there Subway to Conservatory-Central Park Drive (Green Line) | Hours Daily 9am–5pm (Wed until 8pm) | Tip The Elizabeth Morse Genius Children's Garden, located within the conservatory, features climbable leaves, a giant seed pod, a long, curvy slide and best of all, a chance to run around and breathe in oxygen – without a coat, hat, and gloves.

40 Fountain of Youth

Pump your way to vitality

People have been searching the world forever for the magical fountain of youth, the elusive spring that promises to preserve the vigor and vitality of anyone who drinks or bathes in its waters. Conquistador Juan Ponce de León may have searched high and low throughout the New World for the legendary fountain, but he never thought to look in Chicago's Schiller Woods Forest Preserve, located just off Irving Park Road.

On any given day, you will find people lugging their multiple jugs to the creaky, metal, hand-operated pump that allegedly flows with the hallowed waters of well-being and longevity. The mysterious fount, which was first installed in 1945, could use a little rejuvenation itself, as it takes much muscle and a whole lot of squeaking to pull the water up from the extraordinary aquifer located 80-plus feet below the ground.

Though chemical analysis insists this is your typical water from a deep well, ask any bottle-bearing believer here and they'll tell you: this water not only tastes better, but it will make you feel better too. The mineral count is indeed higher than your standard tap water, with markedly low levels of iron and no added fluoride or chlorine. But despite the claims of the pump's faithful followers, no one has been able to determine if the water will keep you alive and kicking forever. It is indeed safe, as it is tested by the Illinois Department of Public Health for potentially harmful bacteria and other contaminants. It also tastes outstanding, with no metallic aftertaste whatsoever, but for a slight, smooth sulfur finish to remind you of its powers.

No matter the season, the weather, or the time of day, the Schiller Woods fountain's faithful are willing to stand in the lengthy line to get their fill of the mysterious waters. Bring a jug or two and get ready to pump your way towards eternal youth.

Address N Cumberland Avenue and W Irving Park Road, www.fpdcc.com/schiller-woods | Getting there Subway to Irving Park (Blue Line) then CTA bus 80 to Cumberland & Irving Park | Tip The Fountain of Youth is located on the south side of Irving Park Road, just west of Cumberland Avenue. After you've loaded up on longevity, head over to the model airplane flying field, just east of the fountain, where enthusiasts wield not just small-scale planes but also UFO-like drones and helicopters.

41 Fountain Girl

Water not whisky

Turn-of-the-century Chicago was a boozing and brawling city. A group of women, sick and tired of dealing with all the drinking, banded together to form the Woman's Christian Temperance Union (WCTU). They fought to provide groundbreaking social services to women who had to suffer from the fallout from chronic alcoholism. They established lodging houses, daycare centers for children of working women, a medical dispensary, kindergartens and Sunday schools – all groundbreaking public services at a time when heavy drinking was almost the norm among the working class. Though they were not strictly prohibitionist, the union did fight for social-reform agendas related to liquor. In a quiet corner of Lincoln Park, a bronze statue of a little girl offering water is a reminder of the struggle these women endured in the face of rampant alcohol abuse. The women's very own children saved up their pennies and nickels to pay for the Fountain Girl.

Water trickles down from the Fountain Girl's bronze cup, which resembles the badge of the Temperance Union, into a stone basin below. Horses once lapped up the water from the basin; today it is a popular spot for thirsty dogs.

The Fountain Girl's innocence, portrayed in her simple dress and bare feet, betray her true age and background. The 4.5-foot-tall little girl has moved around the city several times and even went missing for a spell that lasted 60 years. Her first job was to provide a healthy alternative to liquor – fresh water – to visitors at the World's Columbian Exposition in 1893. She lived in Jackson Park, the Loop, and then Lincoln Park, until she was stolen in 1958. The Chicago Park District tracked down a copy of the statue in Portland, Maine and molded her back into life once again in 2012. She is named in memory of suffragist and noted feminist Frances Willard, who served as the second president of the WCTU.

Address South of W LaSalle Drive and east of Chicago History Museum | Getting there Subway to Sedgwick (Brown and Purple Line) | Tip The Frances Willard House, once the home of Frances Willard and her family as well as was the longtime headquarters of the Woman's Christian Temperance Union, is now a museum dedicated to Willard, one of history's most forward-thinking women (1730 Chicago Avenue, Evanston, IL 60201, +1 (847) 328-7500, www.franceswillardhouse.org).

42_Full Moon Fire Jam

Dancing by the light of the moon

When the full moon appears and looms over Lake Michigan, a fire ignites within the hearts of the creative people who gather on the sandy beach just south of Foster Avenue. Post-sunset, fire dancers light up the beach to the beat of the gathered percussionists; blazing poi, staffs, and hula hoops mesmerize the fans of the bewitching Full Moon Fire Jam, a magical, moonlit reverie. If you can't make it out to Black Rock City, the Full Moon Fire Jam that unfolds along the sandy beach is as close as you'll get to the Burning Man in Chicago.

What started in 2004 with a group of friends coming together to celebrate a birthday has grown into a free monthly celebration that draws one of the most diverse crowds in the city. The mission sounds lofty – "to unite performing artists and spectators through a love and appreciation of fire art" – but the end product is a friendly jam that goes beyond its main objective by uniting people of all ages, backgrounds and interests, from local Burners to casual passersby who find themselves mesmerized by the melding of artistry and athleticism that is performance fire art.

Full Moon Fire Jams take place on the night of each full moon falling between Sundays and Thursdays, from late spring to late fall. Performances take place south of the Foster Avenue Turf Fields, on the lakefront near the 5100 block of N Lake Shore Drive. They begin at sundown and end at 10pm. The jams are volunteer-run, not-for-profit, free to attend, family- and pet-friendly gatherings that follow the "Ten Principles of Burning Man": radical inclusion, gifting, decommodification, radical self-reliance, radical self-expression, communal effort, civic responsibility, "leave no trace," participation, and immediacy. Be sure to arrive early to secure a space. And bring water, blankets, your positive energy and a djembe if you want to join the jam session.

Address Lakefront, near 5100 Block of N Lakeshore Drive, www.fullmoonjam.org | Getting there Subway to Argyle (Red Line) | Hours Late spring–late fall; on full moon nights falling Sun–Thu, sunset–10pm | Tip If you want to learn how to dance with fire, literally, Pyrotechniq Chicago offers both small and large group workshops as well as private lessons in the fine art of fire spinning in their flow dojos across the city (+1 (773) 682-7777, www.pyrotechniq.org/fire-dancing-lessons).

43_Galos Caves

Seaside therapy in the city

Even in the middle of a cold Chicago winter, guests lounge on chaises and dig their feet into the pebbly ground, while children build castles with buckets and shovels at this uniquely Chicago spa-like spot. The hint of salt sweetens the air.

But this is no summer day at the North Avenue Beach. It is an artificial cave – the first salt-iodine cave in the United States – and it's hidden just off the hustle and bustle that is Irving Park Road, nestled beneath the Jolly Inn Banquet Hall.

Eastern Europeans have touted the health benefits of salt therapy, a.k.a. halotherapy, for decades, and the Polish community of Chicago ushered in its very own Chicago-style cave, designed to mimic the real salt caves of Kraków, in the early 2000s. Many believe that these salty spaces alleviate a range of ailments, from arthritis to allergies.

You'll be given a pair of fresh white socks before you enter the "cave," a peaceful, pastel-lit room lined from top to bottom with Dead Sea salt. Faux stalactites hang from the ceiling; seashells decorate the walls. A column features dancing dolphins and a small ceramic mermaid sits in a corner. The ground is about four inches thick with large salt crystals. Kids play with the salt crystals – sand toys are provided – while adults tend to fall asleep to the soft, relaxing seaside soundtrack in the comfy lounge chairs. Visitors are asked to remain quiet during each 45-minute cave session, and many find themselves in a meditative state within minutes.

The cave's manager contends that one 45-minute session is equivalent to a three-day trip to the seaside. Is it the vaporized salt or the tranquil atmosphere that leaves guests so relaxed and reinvigorated? Whether the health claims prove true for you or not, you can count on a safe, de-stressing day in the cave that's good for your health, too, so long as you don't eat the salt.

Address 6501 W Irving Park Road, Chicago, IL 60634, +1 (773) 283-7701, www.galoscaves.com | Getting there Subway to Irving Park (Blue Line) then CTA bus 80 to Irving Park & Natchez | Hours Daily 9am–9pm | Tip After your salt cave adventure, head upstairs and dig into Jolly Inn's famous Polish American buffet. With over 24 dishes, a grand salad bar, roasts fresh from the oven, and delightful pastries, this hearty, $9.95, all-you-can-eat Polish buffet is a true gut-buster.

44_Ghost Church Façade

Halfway home for lost souls

At the corner of 19th and Peoria in Pilsen, an eerie, Old Chicago church beckons any lost souls to enter through its heavy wooden doors for a moment of respite and prayer. If you hear the bell in the 90-foot-tall tower toll, you'll know you've made your way into an altogether more spiritual dimension. Step inside the Ghost Church and you'll discover that there is no actual church behind the façade, rather just a small patch of grass and a few remaining stones from the foundation level that once supported a vibrant church.

The German Gothic script above the entrance lets you know that this was once the Zion Evangelical Lutheran Church. The congregation that built it was founded in Pilsen East in 1850, and then the church itself was built in the 1880s. When the last of the German-American congregants moved out of their East Pilsen neighborhood in 1956, they sold their church. It remained shuttered from the community until a fire in 1979 gutted the interior, and then the walls were knocked down to the ground by a severe windstorm in 1998, leaving little else besides the front façade and the bell tower.

Developer John Podmajersky Jr. purchased the property prior to the windstorm. When a group of descendants of the original congregants visited him, they brought with them an old book written in German that contained the church's early history, and his heartstrings were officially tugged. Podmajersky proceeded to restore the building's original façade and bell tower, and he has maintained the ghostly church ever since. He has plans to turn the bell tower into 10 small studio spaces.

Though the sanctuary itself is gone, it is still possible to sit upon the foundation stones to contemplate life prayerfully, in front of the still charred statue of Christ that remains high on the back of the bare brick, steel-truss supported entrance wall.

Address 19th Street and S Peoria Street, Chicago, IL 60608 | Getting there Subway to 18th (Pink Line) or CTA bus 62 to Halsted & 18th Street | Tip Kitty-corner from the Ghost Church you'll find Open Books, a browse worthy, nonprofit secondhand bookstore for kids and adults, with all proceeds dedicated to supporting community literacy programs (905 W 19th Street., www.open-books.org).

45_Glessner House

Upstairs and downstairs at Chicago's own Downton Abbey

It is a scene straight out of Downton Abbey: servants working hard behind the scenes to ensure that the upper-crust family they serve is fully pampered and protected. Though the fortress-like John J. Glessner House, with its monumental stone blocks, round arches, and pink granite walls, was a defined departure from Victorian-style domestic architecture, the operation of their luxe household required a sizeable live-in staff in days gone by. The servants' quarters of this magnificent home offer a glimpse into Gilded Age Chicago, an era when rich early industrialists like John Glessner – a partner in a farm equipment company – lived lives of luxury, albeit Chicago-style, on posh Prairie Avenue.

Completed in 1887, by Paris-trained architect Henry Hobson Richardson, the façade of the home was inspired by another abbey, the English Abingdon Abbey. At 17,000 square feet, it was designed for a family of four and a live-in staff of eight.

Male servants lived above the coach house; female servants above the kitchen. The butler's apartment stands separate from the rest, at the northeast corner of the third floor. Separate male and female wings, corridors and entrances ensured that servants had as little contact as possible with both the family and the opposite sex. They did all dine together in the separate servants' dining room, at the large table where dinner was served early, at 3pm each day, so that they could later prepare dinner for their masters. The annunciator in the kitchen allowed for staff to be called from anywhere in the house at a moment's notice.

Frances Glessner maintained a journal, viewable upon request, that recorded the name of all the servants as they were hired, along with their pay and position, and the reason why they left service or were dismissed, thus inadvertently creating a portrait of the "forgotten" residents of Prairie Avenue.

Address 1800 S Prairie Avenue, Chicago, IL 60616, +1 (312) 326-1480, www.glessnerhouse.org | Getting there Train to 18th Street (Metra Electric Line); CTA bus 3 or 4 to Michigan & 18th Street | Hours Tours, Wed–Sun 11:30am, 1pm, & 2:30pm; maximum 15 people per tour on a first come, first served, walk-in basis | Tip See if you can spot the *ouroboros* (dragons eating their tails), acanthus leaves, and delicate G shapes that appear hidden throughout the exterior and interior of the house.

46_Grainger Hall of Gems

So dazzling you'll want to wear shades

The geological exhibit at the 1893 World's Columbian Exposition dazzled fairgoers, many of whom could never have even imagined seeing such precious gemstones in person, especially the glittering, ultra-rare diamond fixed in its ancient rock home, a.k.a. matrix. After the fair, several prominent Chicagoans, including the industrialist Edward Ayer, convinced the millionaire merchant Marshall Field to fund the establishment of a museum to house the fair's prized and invaluable geological collection. By late 1893, Chicago's Field Museum was incorporated. In the Grainger Hall of Gems, you can still see the same sparkling gemstones that were once on display and delighted the masses at the Columbian Exposition. 600 brilliant stones and 150 pieces of gleaming jewelry shine so brightly you might want to wear sunglasses.

Each display in the Grainger Hall of Gems shows how cherished jewels are born: first, housed in the original, ancient rock matrix in which they were found, then in their cut and polished stone phase, and finally as finished pieces of fine jewelry. The glittering hall also showcases multiple specimens of tanzanite, which is 1,000 times rarer than diamond.

Illustrious Chicagoans including Marshall Field donated most of the gems here, and Harlow Higinbotham, who was one of Field's associates, purchased and donated the fair's extensive collection of pieces from Tiffany & Co. Check out the stunning 148.5-carat aquamarine set in a platinum and gold pin; the brooch centered by a 500-plus-year-old Mexican opal; the world's largest and rarest ruby topaz at 97.5 carats; the one-of-a-kind, color changing chrysoberyl alexandrite; and the emerald necklace set in 14-karat yellow gold and featuring 18 emeralds and 238 brilliant-cut diamonds, totaling 14.75 carats. All are as enthralling today as they first were at the Exposition over a century ago.

Address The Field Museum, 1400 S Lake Shore Drive, Chicago, IL 60605, +1 (773) 684-1414, www.fieldmuseum.org | Getting there Subway to Roosevelt (Green, Orange, and Red Line) | Hours Daily 9am–5pm | Tip Jewelry lovers will also want to visit the Elizabeth Hubert Malott Hall of Jades, a permanent display of more than 450 objects that will take you on a walk through China's history, from prehistoric burials through two thousand years of the world's most enduring empire.

47 Gwendolyn Brooks' Outdoor Office

The oracle of Bronzeville

In 1967, Richard Daley, then mayor of Chicago, asked Gwendolyn Brooks to write a poem to commemorate the dedication of the *Chicago Picasso*, the enormous, often misunderstood, pigeon-like steel sculpture that still stands in Daley Plaza downtown. Her poem is perhaps best remembered for the line, "Art urges voyages – and it is easier to stay at home."

Gwendolyn Brooks chose the more difficult path – to create the art that urges voyages – as she captured the vitality of her beloved neighborhood, Bronzeville, the cultural hub of Black America, throughout her prolific writing career.

Born in Topeka, Kansas on June 7, 1917, Brooks was raised in Chicago and lived here until her death on December 3, 2000. A prolific writer, she was the author of more than twenty books of poetry, including *Children Coming Home* (The David Co., 1991); *Annie Allen* (Harper, 1949), for which she received the Pulitzer Prize; and *A Street in Bronzeville* (Harper & Brothers, 1945). She also wrote a novel, *Maud Martha* (Harper, 1953) and a memoir, *Report from Part One: An Autobiography* (Broadside Press, 1972). In 1968, she was named Poet Laureate for the State of Illinois, and in 1985, she was the first Black woman appointed as Consultant in Poetry to the Library of Congress, a post now known as United States Poet Laureate.

This new park, inaugurated in 2018 and located less than one mile from her childhood home at 4332 South Champlain, celebrates Brooks, "the oracle of Bronzeville," and includes a sculpted bust of Brooks, a stepping stone path etched with quotations from *Annie Allen*, and a stone circle. Step into her "outdoor office," and take a moment to sit on the porch modeled after the poet's childhood writing spot for a glimpse into Brooks' unique perspective on Bronzeville.

Address 4532 S Greenwood Avenue, Chicago, IL 60653, +1 (312) 747-7138, www.chicagoparkdistrict.com/parks-facilities/brooks-gwendolyn-park | Getting there Metra to 47th St. (Kenwood) | Hours Daily dawn–dusk | Tip While in Bronzeville, pay a visit to the Monument to the Great Northern Migration (345 E Eastgate Place, Chicago, IL 60616). Sculptor Alison Saar created this bronze figure as a testament to the thousands of African Americans who migrated to Chicago in the early 20th century in search of freedom and opportunity.

48__The Hideout

Hidden watering hole for rebels at heart

Hidden amidst the factories of the Elston Avenue industrial corridor lies a completely out of place, balloon-framed watering hole known as the Hideout. In its 80-plus-year history, everyone from bootleggers to bookies, from undiscovered rock stars to about-to-be-arrested gangsters have sought refuge in this self-described "regular guy bar for irregular folks who just don't fit in, or just don't want to fit in." This is a bar for rebels with an extraordinary appreciation of live music.

There are no signs to indicate that you've arrived at this musical refuge, so look for the retro Old Style plaque glowing just above the incognito front entrance. During Prohibition, the Hideout truly was a hideout for rum runners and gamblers; it never shed its off-the-radar vibe. Inside, exposed wooden beams, records suspended from the ceiling with yarn, and taxidermied marlins recall a mid-century, basement rec room.

At its heart, a small, string-lit stage welcomes acts of all genres – from bluegrass to blues, from rock to reggae, from punk to pop. The Hideout's patrons are known for having refined yet eclectic musical tastes.

Many musical icons find themselves unexpectedly nervous onstage here, knowing full well that the Hideout audience is a tough one to win over no matter how many records you've sold. Up-and-coming performers know they stand a chance if the crowd here acknowledges them with even the slightest applause.

As the website explains, "The Hideout is not your Dad's bar, but your Granddad's bar. It is the bar that Granddad went to when he was young and crazy. He did his best to hide that past from your Dad, but you have found it. The old, restless roots of hard-working, hard-playing creative artistic expression and intellectual freedom. More New Deal and less New Age. The Hideout is small, and small is beautiful. It's not for everyone, but for every one."

Address 800 S Halsted Street, Chicago, IL 60607, +1 (312) 413-5353, www.hullhousemuseum.org | **Getting there** Subway to UIC-Halsted (Blue Line) | **Hours** Tue–Fri 10am–4pm; Sun noon–4pm | **Tip** Public tours every Wednesday and Sunday at 1pm are led by museum educators and last one hour. Meet in the entryway of the Hull House. No reservations are necessary; tours are free but donations to the museum are encouraged.

50_Iwan Ries & Co.

Where King Tobacco still reigns

Chicago was once a smoking town, where most every man, rich or poor, cherished a long drag on a good cigar or pipe packed with fragrant tobacco. Today you would be hard pressed to find anyone smoking inside even the grittiest bar, thanks to the 2008 Smoke Free Illinois Act. But there is one secret Loop lounge where you can puff away to your heart's (dis)content on some of the finest tobacco blends in the world. At Iwan Ries' swanky lounge, cigars have staged their comeback, and pipe smoking is a practice that has never gone out of style.

Iwan Ries and Company has supplied smokers with tobacco, pipes, lighters, and many more accoutrements since 1857, making it the oldest family-owned tobacco shop in the country. Prepare to be enveloped in the heady smell of fine cigar and pipe tobacco as soon as the elevator opens to reveal this second-floor shop, located in the Adler and Sullivan designed Jewelers Building (1881). Rows upon rows of cigars line the glass cases, while over 15,000 pipes are displayed on the walls, include a noteworthy collection of antique pipes, snuff boxes, and lighters. Among the many different types of tobacco, the shop's signature blend – Three Star Blue – stands apart from all of the others.

Step into the private smoking lounge, sink into a leather chair, and take in both the fine tobacco and the fine views of bustling Wabash Avenue below, and the L as it snakes its way around the Loop before your eyes. The lounge managed to be grandfathered in when the city smoking ban went into effect, and hence stands as downtown Chicago's one and only smoking lounge. You can pay for a single entrance, or you can become a member for a marvelous set of benefits, including personal key-card access and invitations to private tastings and events. The lounge is BYOB, so bring a bottle of your favorite cognac or port; glassware is provided.

Address 19 S Wabash Avenue, Chicago, IL 60603, +1 (312) 372-1306, www.iwanries-hub.com | **Getting there** Subway to Monroe (Red Line) or Randolph/Wabash (Brown, Green, Orange, Pink, and Purple Line) | **Hours** Mon–Fri 9am–5:30pm; Sat 9am–5pm | **Tip** Chicago's landmark Jewelers Row spans two blocks of Wabash Avenue, between E Washington Street and E Monroe Street, making it the most popular spot to choose a cherished engagement ring. At the Jewelers Center housed in the Mallers Building, a magnificent Art Deco structure built in 1912, you'll find over 180 independent jewelers under one roof (5 S Wabash Avenue, www.jewelerscenter.com).

51 Johnny Weissmuller Pool

Tarzan's training grounds

The Medinah Athletic Club opened its doors in 1929 to much acclaim. Private and exclusive, this tony club was a posh playground for Chicago's rising rich and famous crowd. Over $5 million had been spent building the club's extravagant, Assyrian-inspired building, which stood at 42 stories and was capped with a Moorish-style golden dome, built to serve as a docking port for dirigibles. A miniature golf course, shooting range, billiard hall, running track, gymnasium, archery range, bowling alley, and a two-story boxing arena challenged the club's 3,000 members. On the 14th floor, the Johnny Weissmuller Pool shined, an Art Deco gem reminiscent of the Golden Age in Spain.

Best known for swinging into the role of Tarzan on the silver screen in the thirties and forties, Johnny Weissmuller was also a competitive swimmer with a number of records under his belt. When in Chicago, the Hollywood dreamboat dove into the exclusive swimming pool now named in his honor.

Ten feet at its deepest end, the pool's diving board is long gone, but you can still dive in and swim laps or just cool off after a busy day of shopping the Magnificent Mile. Note the tin-glazed majolica tiles that line the blue-tiled pool's edge. In keeping with the marine motif, the terracotta statue of Neptune on the eastern wall is surrounded by wide-mouthed fish fountains. When light shines through the windows with their scale-shaped aquamarine and sapphire stained glass, schools of fish are magically reflected onto the water.

Swimming was once a popular spectator sport, so order a retro cocktail and lie back on one of the poolside wicker chaise lounges and imagine watching synchronized swimming icon Ester Williams gracefully diving in before your eyes, as she did in the 1940s, when the Johnny Weissmuller Pool was one of the most glamorous places to see and be seen in the city.

Address InterContinental Chicago, 505 N Michigan Avenue, Chicago, IL 60611, +1 (312) 944-4100, www.icchicagohotel.com | Getting there Subway to Grand (Red Line) | Hours Mon–Fri 6am–10pm; Sat & Sun 7am–10pm | Tip Head under N Michigan Avenue to the Billy Goat Tavern for post-swim beers and "Cheezborger, cheezborger, cheezborger, no fries, chips," a line immortalized by John Belushi in "Olympia Café," a hilarious *Saturday Night Live* sketch inspired by the tavern (430 N Michigan Avenue, lower level, www.billygoattavern.com).

52__Kusanya Cafe

A cup of Joe with a side of community

Chicago's Englewood neighborhood, best known outside of Chicago as the setting for Spike Lee's *Chi-Raq*, is plagued with violence. With 46.6 percent of households in this South Side neighborhood living below the poverty line, a 28 percent unemployment rate, an overall crime rate that reaches 105 percent higher than the national average, and a grim murder rate, the highest in the city of Chicago, Englewood's reputation makes it tough for local businesses to prosper. Yet hope still grows in Englewood. Kusanya Cafe, a rustic-chic non-profit cafe, roaster, and gallery housed in a 100-plus-year-old building, offers a sense of community, a slice of peace, and a whole lot of love with every cup of Joe served at the cost of merely $1.

When Phil Sipka and some of his Englewood neighbors opened the small cafe in 2013, they made a point of being vulnerable in this corner of the city that struggles to shed its violent exterior. There would be no onsite security guards, no security gates, no protective window screens. Instead they set out to be a safe place where everyone is not only welcomed but embraced and offered sustenance with kindness and friendship on a daily basis. Fittingly, Kusanya is a Swahili word that means "to gather."

In addition to serving freshly roasted and expertly brewed coffee, all-day breakfast, and sandwiches, Kusanya is home to a variety of free, community-driven arts, culture, and educational events, including Saturday morning yoga, and an open mic for storytellers from the neighborhood and the city every second Saturday. Paintings from local artists line the exposed brick walls.

Kusanya Cafe is a sit and stay a while, "for-here-mug" kind of place. Expect casual interactions among neighbors and chance meetings. Prepare to go behind the headlines and have your preconceived opinions and/or fears surrounding Englewood shattered as you walk through the door.

Address 825 W 69th Street, Chicago, IL 60621, +1 (773) 675-4758, www.kusanyacafe.org | Getting there Subway to 69th (Red Line) | Hours Mon–Sat 7am–5pm | Tip On the second Saturday of every month, Kusanya Cafe opens the mic to storytellers from around the neighborhood and across the city for its 'Do Not Submit' series. Signup list at 3pm, stories begin at 3:30pm. You have seven minutes to tell your tale.

53_Leather Archives and Museum

Capturing a scintillating subculture

It holds one of the most interesting collections of artifacts in the city of Chicago, stands as the first and foremost museum of its kind, promises to provoke, challenge and engage – and yet few people even know that this fascinating museum exists. The Leather Archives and Museum delves deep into the fascinating BDSM culture and community. Its 10,000-square-foot building, located in Rogers Park, houses eight exhibitions, an extensive archival storage space, an auditorium, a library, and, of course, a veritable sex dungeon in its basement. The focus here is on bondage, discipline (or domination), sadism, and masochism (as a type of sexual practice), and on the leather subculture in all its glorious forms of expression. Many displayed treasures mark the subculture's journey out of the closet, from early beefcake mags to the flag carried by the Leather Contingent at the 25th anniversary of the Stonewall Riot in New York City.

Leather culture sprouted up out of biker culture in the 1940s, when devotees dressed in leather garments – boots, chaps, harnesses, jackets – to separate themselves from the mainstream. The culture has found different expressions within the gay, lesbian, bisexual, and straight worlds, but it's most visible in gay communities. In addition to boasting the first leather museum of its kind in the world, Chicago plays host to the annual International Mr. Leather, the largest leather conference and contest in the world. The Windy City was also the home of the first gay leather bar, the Gold Coast, which opened its doors and many closed minds way back in 1958.

While many of the objects on display here lean towards the titillating – antique whips, chains, spanking machines, handcuffs, vintage leather fetish clothing – the stately museum is also home to extensive archives that document the history of this captivating counterculture.

Address 6418 N Greenview Avenue, Chicago, IL 60626, +1 (773) 761-9200, www.leatherarchives.org | Getting there Subway to Loyola (Red Line) | Hours Thu–Fri 11am–7pm, Sat & Sun 11am–5pm | Tip Touché began welcoming leather lovers way back in 1977, and it remains one of the best leather fetish bars in the city (6412 N Clark Street, www.touchechicago.com).

54_Leopard-Print House

Ferocious façade

Roger's Park is known for its artsy vibe. A few of the houses in this eclectic neighborhood march to the beat of their own design drum. There's the junk home at 1790 W Lunt Avenue, with its front yard packed with a well-intentioned mix of … junk, and the Candyland House at 1525 W Pratt Boulevard, which is painted all the sweet, pastel shades of the Hasbro board game (owner Jackie Seiden was inspired by the colored deco style of the now defunct Edgewater Beach Hotel). The Leopard House at 1623 W Estes Avenue features the most ferocious façade of all.

Love it or hate it, Rogers Park's one and only leopard-print home is striking, like a wild animal trying to blend into the city of Chicago but falling terribly flat. Between the tamer homes on W Estes Avenue, it sits, both regally and comically, a finger in the face of gentrification and failed efforts at fitting in. When the residents here unofficially listed the wild home for sale on April 1, 2007, they took great joy in pronouncing "April Fools'!" as eager developers waltzed in the door eyeing an impossible deal.

Officially named the "Roger Spark Presents Wes Testes's Faerie Castle: Asbestos-on-Estes," it's more commonly referred to as the Castle or the Leopard-Print House, which may actually be a misnomer as no one has confirmed whether the print is that of a leopard, a cheetah, a jaguar, or perhaps even a giraffe. Many wild parties were hosted here in its early, undomesticated days. Don't let the ferocious façade fool you – this home is as quiet as an elderly house cat.

Fifteen years ago, the original six residents couldn't come up with a consensus on an exterior paint color but they all agreed that a funky wild animal print would fit the bill. Is it garish or gorgeously offbeat? You decide. One thing is for certain: it's easy to spot this wild beast of a home among the tamer, more sedate W Estes Avenue residences.

Address 1623 W Estes Avenue, Chicago, IL 60626 | **Getting there** Subway to Morse (Red Line) | **Tip** Moah's Ark is an urban farm complete with extensive chicken coops, nestled between two two-flat apartment buildings. You'll know you're approaching if you hear a friendly cock-a-doodle-do or spot a wandering rooster (1839 W Touhy Avenue).

55_Light Court at the Rookery

Illuminating from within

When it opened in 1885, the 11-story Rookery was seen as a soaring skyscraper, an engineering marvel. This once-tallest building in the city of Chicago cost a whopping $1.5 million and was considered the most elegant office building in the country. To this day, it remains a most sought-after address within the LaSalle Street financial corridor, and it stands as the oldest high-rise in the city. Step into the glorious, two-story light court with its glass ceiling, white-glazed brick walls, sublime light fixtures, and winding oriel staircase, and you'll see why it's considered one of architect Frank Lloyd Wright's grandest masterpieces. It was also his first major architectural job, and his only remaining work in downtown Chicago.

The Rookery's interior light court illuminates the building's square interior, designed by famed 19th-century Chicago architects John Wellborn Root and Daniel Burnham in 1888. Wright was hired in 1905 to remodel the steel-laden, glass-ceiling topped lobby. He added all his meticulous, Prairie-style touches, including luxurious white marble with Persian-style ornamentation, intricate staircase railings, ornamented light fixtures, and the signature, decorative urns at the base of the staircase, creating a modernized design that maximized available light. Walk up the curving, heavily ornamented staircase which winds up from the 2nd floor, wrap-around balcony to the 12th floor, and you'll see why the light court at the Rookery was a place to see and be seen at the turn of the century.

The Rookery was named after the many pigeons and crows, a.k.a. rooks, that set up their nests on the building's exterior, and the shady politicians who worked in the post-fire City Hall that once stood on the site. See if you can spot the couple of rooks carved on the façade over the LaSalle Street entrance by architect John Root.

Address 209 S LaSalle Street, Chicago, IL 60604, +1 (312) 553-6100, www.therookerybuilding.com | **Getting there** Subway to Quincy/Wells (Brown, Orange, Pink, and Purple Line) | **Hours** Mon–Fri 6am–6pm; Sat 6am–2pm | **Tip** You might recognize the Rookery from *Home Alone 2: Lost in New York*, in which the exterior and one of the lower levels were modeled as the toy store, "Duncan's Toy Chest." The building also starred in the 1987 film *The Untouchables* as the police headquarters of Eliot Ness.

56_LondonHouse Cupola

Pop the question at the tiptop

If you are going to pop the question, do it here, 23 stories above street level in the open-air, cozy cupola of a landmark 1920s skyscraper. Majestic 360-degree views of the Chicago River and downtown will surround you as you toast to a new life together and sip champagne in the most exclusive private dining spot in the city.

Designed by Chicago architect Alfred S. Alschuler, the Beaux Arts London Guarantee & Accident Building stands at the south bank of the Chicago River, on the former site of Fort Dearborn. The fort itself was built in 1808 and played an important role in early Chicago history, as witness to a major battle in 1812. You will see a bronze relief depicting the famous fort above the building's main entrance on East Wacker Drive. Restored to its former glory and transformed into the LondonHouse Hotel in 2013, the property sold in 2016 for a cool $315 million, making it the highest per-room ever paid for a Chicago hotel, at $697,000 per room. The hotel's name is a tribute to the famous, eponymous first-floor nightclub that hosted some of the biggest names in jazz from the fifties through the early seventies.

The temple-like circular cupola, raised on an elaborate podium at the tipy top, is reminiscent of the glorious Choragic Monument of Lysicrates in Athens. Ringed with regal columns and capped with a cupola inscribed with an X and O pattern that is part of its original 1923 design, the intimate terrace seats only two. It seems to have been designed with romance in mind, making it Chicago's premier proposal site. The $1,000 price tag to rent this timeless perch includes everything you need to pop the question: a kneeler, a bottle of Dom Perignon, and a discount on a wedding, should you choose to celebrate your nuptials at the LondonHouse. A beaming "Yes!" is not guaranteed, but a starry night sky and glittering city lights are added bonuses.

Address 85 E Upper Wacker Drive, Chicago, IL 60601, +1 (312) 357-1200, www.londonhousechicago.com | **Getting there** Subway to State/Lake (Brown, Green, Orange, Pink, and Purple Line) | **Hours** By reservation only | **Tip** The nearby Jewelers Building once featured car elevators that whisked jewelers concerned with their safety to private, secure parking garages on the lower 23 floors. During Prohibition, the building's magnificent dome held Al Capone's speakeasy, the Stratosphere Club. Check out the building's creepy corner clock, attached to the Wacker Drive façade, which features Father Time and his devilish scythe, outlined in blood-red light bulbs (35 E Wacker Drive).

57 Lost Lincoln Bust

I'm still standing

If you've ever wandered the streets of Englewood, you've likely encountered a five-foot-tall, alabaster bust, serious and stately despite its timeworn facial features. For years the bust lived on the corner 69th Street and Wolcott Avenue. Every once in awhile he was known to vanish, only to resurface in yet another random, neighborhood spot. Before he found his most recent home in the courtyard of the West Englewood Library, the bust lived in a muddy CDOT maintenance yard.

Once upon a time, the Lincoln Gas Station stood on that same corner. In 1926, owner Philip Bloomquist commissioned a statue of none other than the nation's 16th president to advertise his fledgling business. It certainly caught people's attention. Time passed, and the Lincoln Gas Station was closed, then torn down. Still, the bust of Lincoln refused to leave the neighborhood ... for almost ninety years. The Gangster Disciples made use of him to mark their territory. Over the years he's been tagged and coated in paint. His nose broke off, turning him into a sort of South Side sphinx.

The Lost Lincoln Bust simply can't compare to Augustus Saint-Gaudens' larger-than-life Standing Lincoln, considered one of the most famous statues in Chicago. Unveiled in Lincoln Park in 1887, the New York Evening Post called it "the most important achievement American sculpture has yet produced." Located near Belden Avenue and Cannon Drive, the statue of a contemplative Lincoln rising from a chair inspired replicas that still stand proudly around the world (including a copy in London's Parliament Square).

But the Lost Lincoln Bust remains a stalwart part of the neighborhood, and the community recently pushed to secure him a safer home. Although the elements have worn down his distinct features, he still commands respect after all these years from his new, courtyard perch in the West Englewood Library.

Address 1745 W 63rd Street, Chicago, IL 60636, www.chipublib.org/locations/76, +1 (312) 747-3481 | Getting there Subway to 63rd (Red Line) | Hours Mon & Wed noon–8pm, Tue & Thu 10am–6pm, Fr & Sat 9am–5pm | Tip Be sure to check out the two works by local artists showcased in this same vibrant library. Artist Ian Weaver's Barack Obama and The Principles of Courage and Hope (2009) incorporates traditional Kente fabric to show the strong connection between President Obama and Chicago's South Side community. Artist David Philpot's three intricately hand-carved walking sticks in Essence of the Universe (1991) symbolize the three pillars of leadership, power and community (www.chipublib.org/about-west-englewood-branch).

58_Maggie Daley Park Skating Ribbon

The cherry atop winter's cake

Gliding on the Maggie Daley Park Skating Ribbon is the cherry atop winter's cake. Merry skaters zoom along the quarter-mile-long, 20-foot-wide rink, while beginners hold tight to rails to make their skating experience a bit easier on the behind. This is the most beautiful spot in the city to skate your winter worries away and experience the joys of the season, especially in the evening, when the city's skyscrapers glow with holiday lights, the stars twinkle overhead, and the chill makes holding mittened hands with your loved ones not so much a necessity but a joy.

Located near the Lake Michigan shoreline in northeastern Grant Park, the 20-acre park, inaugurated in 2014, was named for Maggie Daley, the beloved former first lady of the city who died in 2011. The park features tennis courts, perhaps the most amazing playground in the city, picnic groves, and gorgeous gardens. In the summer, new and experienced climbers test their skills on the rock-climbing structures, which reach up to 40 feet. In the wintertime, the ribbon rink is abuzz with skaters. The many smiling kids that visit this city park are a happy reminder of Maggie Daley's love and hard work on behalf of Chicago's children.

Skate around the loop – twice the length of a lap around a traditional skating rink – then warm up with some hot cocoa in the adjacent warming house. The rink is closed for one-hour periods, during which the ice is resurfaced by a rambling Zamboni machine. Thankfully, this zesty Zamboni has a dedicated twitter account, @MDPZamboni, so you can make sure to arrive when the ice is at its smoothest.

When spring arrives and the ice melts away, the skating ribbon morphs into a paved, winding walking path where visitors are welcome to whiz around on roller skates.

Address 337 E Randolph Street, Chicago, IL 60601, +1 (312) 552-3000, www.chicagoparkdistrict.com/parks | Getting there Train to Millennium Station (Metra Electric and South Shore Line); subway to Randolph/Wabash (Brown, Green, Orange, Pink, and Purple Line) | Hours Mon–Thu noon–8pm; Fri noon–10pm; Sat 10am–10pm; Sun 10am–8pm | Tip Post-ice skating, warm up with hot cocoa and upscale American comfort food at the Tavern at the Park. In the summer time, you'll want to sip cocktails on the second-story outdoor patio which overlooks Millennium Park (130 E Randolph Street, Chicago, IL 60601, www.tavernonthepark.com).

59 The Magic Hedge

Ornithophiles' paradise

Blackburnian warblers and black-headed gulls. Snowy owls and saw-whets. Black-bellied plovers and semi-palmated sparrows. When these rare birds fly over Lake Michigan, they usually swoop down, stop, and stay for a while at a magical 15-acre lakeside sanctuary, where thick hedgerows, trees with hospitable branches, and dense thickets act as a five-star Chicago hotel for the birds.

Many birds love the Montrose Point Bird Sanctuary, also known as the Magic Hedge, a small tree- and bush-packed finger that pokes out into Lake Michigan. Over 300 species of birds have been spotted on this unofficial Chicago landing pad for our feathered friends. Located along a natural migratory corridor, this phenomenal hedge almost magically attracts birds as the first natural cover that southbound migrant birds hit after flying the 307-mile length of Lake Michigan. But it likely earned its nickname from the many human visitors that enjoy toking on other mystifying herbs among the peaceful, secluded greenery.

In the spring and fall, the Magic Hedge bustles with avian activity, as migrating birds stop to refuel at this natural reserve. Early in the morning, when the rising sun awakens the insects, you will find plenty of birds on the prowl at the breakfast buffet. Take a walk out on the nearby pier, where loons and long-tailed ducks like to linger. In the wintertime, scan the snow-blanketed sand for the elusive and beautiful snowy owls that have been making more frequent Magic Hedge appearances in the past few years. Keep your eyes on the skies, and you just might spot a swooping peregrine falcon.

The Magic Hedge can be found by following Montrose Avenue east, crossing Lake Shore Drive and making your way towards Lincoln Park's lakefront. Take a right at the street next to the bait shop. Follow the curve until you spot the ornithophiles' paradise on your left.

Address 4400 N Simonds Avenue, Chicago, IL 60613 | Getting there Subway to Lawrence (Red Line) then CTA bus 81 to Marine Drive & Wilson | Tip Cricket Hill, located just west of the Magic Hedge, is a popular site for kite flying, thanks to its tree-free gentle slope. Every May, kids step out into the sunshine and harness Chicago's wind power at the hill's Kids & Kites Festival (www.chicagokite.com), an annual tradition established by former mayor and kite enthusiast Richard M. Daley.

60_Magic Inc.

Supplier to magicians and mentalists

Professional smoking thumbs, double-backed decks of Bicycle cards, comprehensive guides to mind control, helix devil sticks, French arm choppers, Insta-snakes, squirting lapel roses – you'll find every trick of the magic trade at Magic Inc., a storied Chicago shop stocked with every prop and put-on you can imagine. This full-service magic shop, where the staff members are all magicians, supplies professional magicians and mentalists. It also doubles as an academy for magicians-in-training.

From the late 19th century to the Roaring Twenties, Chicago brimmed with magicians. Most came to the rapidly growing city to make their magical marks at the 1893 World's Columbian Exposition, then stayed to perform in vaudeville theaters, shops, and taverns, and even on street corners.

Famed Chicago magician Laurie L. Ireland, best known for pulling incredible objects out of his jacket sleeves, opened his L. L. Ireland Magic Co. in 1926, when Chicago was already an established magic epicenter. Later he married fellow magician Frances Ahrens Vandevier, founder of the Magigals, a society of lady magicians. Laurie died in 1954, and Frances took over the shop, later marrying Jay Marshall, a noted ventriloquist. They moved the shop to a new location and renamed it Magic Inc. The shop remains in the family today. Jay Marshall's son Alexander "Sandy" Marshall, a theatrical producer living in New York City and two-time Emmy Award winner, splits his time between NYC and Chicago to maintain the family magic business.

If you're considering a career change, take a class – for new as well as experienced magicians. A small theater in the rear of the shop gives budding magicians the chance to test new acts onstage. Magic manuals galore will guide you through literally every trick in the book, while shop staff are happy to demo tools and tricks of the trade.

Address 1838 W Lawrence Avenue, Chicago, IL 60640, +1 (773) 334-2855, www.magicinc.net | Getting there Subway to Damen (Brown Line) | Hours Mon–Thu noon–6pm; Fri noon–7pm; Sat 10:30am–5:30pm; Sun noon–5pm | Tip Third-generation Chicago magician extraordinaire Dennis Watkins performs an intimate evening of classic magic on Friday and Saturday evenings at his Magic Parlor in Chicago's historic Palmer House Hotel. Advance reservations are required, at www.themagicparlourchicago.com.

61_Maxwell Street Market

Where cash is still king

If you are looking for a bargain with a side of history, Chicago's Maxwell Street Market delivers an international, eclectic range of merchandise, with vendors offering everything from used tires to tamales to trinkets. Its essence has not changed much since it was established in the 1840s. For decades, this vibrant market has served as the launching pad for budding entrepreneurs looking to grab their slice of the American pie.

The market first popped up on Maxwell Street, a wooden plank road that ran from the south branch of the Chicago River west to Blue Island Avenue in the 1840s. Newly arrived immigrants – Germans, Irish, Poles, Bohemians, and people of the Jewish faith, many of whom had escaped czarist Russia – declared cash their king and started their business empires from atop folding tables or rickety pushcarts. The market soon became known as a place where you could find just about anything you needed, either new or secondhand, legal or illegal, and at a steep discount.

African Americans arrived on the scene to make their fortunes during the Great Migration, and the market became known for its street entertainers. The need to amplify their sounds over the clamor of the market produced a new musical genre, the electrified, urban "Chicago Blues" that came to define the city. Yet another new wave of immigrants brought their goods to the market in the 1980s and 1990s. Today's predominantly Mexican-American Maxwell Street Market offers some the best Mexican and Latin American street food in the country.

The construction of the Dan Ryan Expressway (I-90/94) and the expansion of the University of Illinois at Chicago displaced the market to its current South Loop location at 800 S Desplaines Street. Though it is smaller in size than the original, the Maxwell Street Market remains a place to make a deal while indulging in street food and music.

Address 800 S Desplaines Street, Chicago, IL 60607, +1 (312) 745-4676, www.cityofchicago.org | **Getting there** Subway to Clinton (Blue Line) | **Hours** Sun 7am–3pm | **Tip** Manny's Coffee Shop & Deli arrived on the Maxwell Street Market scene shortly after World War II, and it remains one of the best spots in the city for good old-fashioned Jewish-American cooking, served up quickly in hearty proportions. Photos, news clippings, and other memorabilia from the market and deli in their early days line the dining room walls (1141 S Jefferson Street, www.mannysdeli.com).

62_McCormick Bridgehouse

Step inside an iconic Chicago bridge

If you are lucky, you might catch the spectacle that takes place, like clockwork, twice a year: in spring, the glorious, moveable bridges of Chicago are raised, one by one, in synchronized succession, from the south to the north and finally to the east, as boats come happily out of storage and head to their Lake Michigan harbors for boating season. In the fall, the iconic bridges open gradually once again, serenading the boats back to dry storage for the winter. If you happen to be walking across a Chicago bridge when the lifting signal sounds, just make sure to run as fast as you can to the other side.

Chicago has more movable bridges than any other city in the world. In downtown Chicago alone, there are 20 movable bridges, which open over 30,000 times throughout the year as more than 50,000 boats travel smoothly down the river. It takes about eight minutes to raise and lower a Chicago-style drawbridge.

Part of the revolutionary 1920 double-decker Michigan Avenue (now DuSable) Bridge, the McCormick Bridgehouse and Chicago River Museum gives visitors the chance to step inside an iconic Chicago moveable bridge and watch firsthand as all the large and small gears work elegantly in sync to lift up and let multiple boats pass through. Located on the south end of Michigan Avenue, the 1,400-square-foot museum begins at river level and spirals five stories up. Educational exhibits showcase the history of the river as well as the science and technology behind the lifting bridges spectacle. Climb to the top of the Bridgehouse, where a splendid 360-degree view of both the city and river awaits.

The Bridgehouse is seasonal and open May through October. You will need to make a special reservation to take part in the twice annual lifting of the bridges. Be sure to check the museum's schedule of bridge lifts at bridgehousemuseum.org/bridge-lifts and order tickets in advance.

Address 99 Chicago Riverwalk, Chicago, IL 60601, +1 (312) 977-0227, www.bridgehousemuseum.org | Getting there Subway to State/Lake (Brown, Orange, Purple, Green, and Pink Line) | Hours May–Oct, Thu–Mon 10am–5pm | Tip Chicago's one and only fish hotel is located in the river, beside the McCormick Bridgehouse Hotel. The hotel is actually a floating garden that provides rest and a safe harbor for sunfish, bluegills, carp and other finned friends that pass through the big city to spend the night. See how many fish you can spot mingling in the hotel's seaweed-filled lobby (www.chicagoriver.org/about-us/success-stories/fish-hotel).

63 Merz Apothecary

Dreamy drugstore

Peter Merz, a Chicago pharmacist of Swiss descent, was riding the rising tide of the retail drug industry when he opened his Lincoln Square apothecary in 1875. Catering to new immigrants, Merz was fluent in several languages and fond of concocting Old World remedies, making Merz a go-to place for unconventional medical advice with a side of neighborhood gossip. "We still have a recipe book that has handwritten formulations dating back more than 100 years," shares current Merz owner, Anthony Qaiyum. "This was from the days when doctors would write up a prescription that then had to be compounded by hand."

Peer inside the leaded glass windows and you'll spot all the hallmarks of a classic apothecary from days gone by: tin ceilings, solid oak cabinets stocked with antique pharmacy jars and herb containers, and comfy leather chairs. The elegant wooden shelves are stocked with over 13,000 herbal tea remedies, natural supplements, a huge selection of hard-to-find European body and bath products, essential-oil-based perfumes, traditional shaving equipment, beard-care products and more, plus a well-trained staff eager to match you with the products that will work best for you. Merz also carries the largest collection of natural and luxury soaps from around the world under one roof.

The store remained in the Merz family for 85 years until 1972, when the last of the Merz', Ralph, handed the business over to Abdul Qaiyum, a 26-year-old Indian-born pharmacist. Qaiyum's son Anthony has now filled his dad's shoes, earning the respect of yet another generation of customers.

The staff today collectively speaks seven languages, and just like yesteryear, dishes out alternative medical and unscripted life advice to a new clientele, including newly-arrived immigrants looking for familiar, natural remedies that you can't find at your standard retail drugstore.

Address 4716 N Lincoln Avenue, Chicago, IL 60625, +1 (773) 989-0900, www.merzapothecary.com | Getting there Subway to Western (Brown Line) | Hours Mon–Sat 9am–6pm | Tip Lincoln Square's DANK Haus German American Cultural Center is a cultural hub for German Americans in Chicago, thanks to a wide array of events. The popular Stammtisch Open Haus is a social evening for people who have a mutual interest in German Chicago, held the third Friday of every month, and German Cinema Now offers a chance to view current films from German-speaking countries (with English subtitles) the fourth Friday of each month (4740 N Western Avenue, +1 (773) 561-9181, www.dankhaus.com).

64__Morgan Shoal and Shipwreck

Chicago's sunken treasure

Three hundred feet off the South Side Chicago shoreline at a depth of about twenty feet, a submerged Atlantis teems with life. The 32-acre Morgan Shoal, a limestone shelf unearthed when glaciers gouged the basin of Lake Michigan centuries ago, represents one of the most biodiverse ecologies in the Midwest, confirmed by studies conducted by the nearby Shedd Aquarium. Quagga mussels grip the shoal, while gobies, lake trout, largemouth bass, yellow perch, and the rare isopods – which first made their appearance on our planet during the Paleozoic Era, some 300 million years ago – find their way through the algae-coated nooks and crannies of Chicago's take on the coral reef.

Snorkel out to this underwater ecology, and you won't believe you are in Chicago. On a clear, calm day, visibility can reach about 20 feet, making it easy to spot the many creatures swimming the shallow shoal. Peep your head above the water to break your tropical reverie and take a look at the Chicago skyline that stands in the distance.

Immediately southwest of the Morgan Shoal lie the remains of the Silver Spray, an 1894 excursion ship. In July of 1914, the 109-foot passenger boat was carrying a group of University of Chicago students on their way to tour the steel mills of Northwest Indiana, when it hit the rocky Morgan Shoal and sank. Most of the 109-foot boat was recovered and burned ashore in bonfires, but the boiler and propeller remain in place. When the lake's water levels are low, the boiler of the Silver Spray, often mistaken for a boulder from the shoreline, pokes up out of the water.

It is an easy swim from Morgan Point out to this unofficial wildlife reserve. A mask, snorkel, and fins will make your trip easier, as will a wet suit, because lake water temperatures are decidedly nontropical.

Address Lake Michigan, 300 feet off Morgan Point at E 47th Street and S Lake Shore Drive | Getting there Train to 47th Street Kenwood (Metra Electric Line) | Tip Underwater Safaris rents snorkeling gear and can also arrange for private, guided dives of Morgan Shoal as well as other Lake Michigan wrecks (2950 N Lincoln Avenue, +1 (773) 348-3999, www.uwsafaris.com).

65 Murder Castle Site

Check out any time you like, but you can never leave

H. H. Holmes was the first documented serial killer in U.S. history. An itinerant grifter and bigamist, he arrived in Chicago in 1883 with murder on his mind.

By 1892 he had secretly constructed a complex Murder Castle that masqueraded as a World's Fair hotel. Though the building was mysteriously gutted by fire in 1895 and replaced in 1939 by the U.S. post office that still stands on the site, many find the area charged with paranormal activity to this day.

Nine murders were confirmed during investigations, but it is estimated that over 200 unlucky guests checked in to Holmes' World Fair hotel and never checked out… alive.

Holmes designed his building as a fully-operating murder machine. Though he wasn't a trained architect, he came up with a plan for a three-story home at the corner of 63rd Street and S Wallace Avenue that called for dozens of rooms, hidden chambers, dissection facilities, trap doors, dumbwaiters, a gas chamber, secret stairways, and passages, as well as an elaborate alarm system. The basement contained a complete crematory, with vats for body disposal via quicklime ready to greet the unluckiest of hotel guests.

By constantly hiring and firing construction workers, he was able to keep his macabre vision hidden from the public. His timing was well planned, too: Holmes' Murder Castle was ready for business in 1892, so he could easily find unwitting lodgers looking for housing while attending the nearby World's Columbian Exposition.

On May 7, 1896, Holmes was hanged. Shortly before his death he himself remarked that he had taken on "a satanical cast." Rumors persist about the location being haunted by the boarders that never emerged. Neighbors claim that dogs will cross the street rather than walk adjacent to the building, while others report hearing the ghastly screams of Holmes' torture victims in the dead of night.

Address 63rd Street and S Wallace Avenue, Chicago, IL 60621 | Getting there Subway (Green and Red Line) or train (Metra BNSF Railway Line) to Halsted | Tip Erik Larson's bestselling nonfiction book, *The Devil in the White City*, chronicles Holmes' murderous mindset.

66_Obama's Barber Chair

Presidential trims

Before he became the 44th president of the United States, Barack Obama was just an average Chicagoan, living with his beautiful wife and two daughters in a lovely Georgian revival mansion at 5046 S Greenwood Avenue. He tucked into scrambled eggs, hash browns, and sausage at Valois Cafeteria (1518 E 53rd Street), browsed the dusty shelves of 57th Street Books (1301 E 57th Street), and had his hair cut at the humble Hyde Park Hair Salon.

Since 1927, the salon has catered to men looking for a quality shave and a haircut. Spike Lee, Phil Gates, Devon Hester, Bill Veeck, Suge Knight, and former Chicago mayor Harold Washington were all regulars, and Obama was a loyal patron of more than 17 years. While serving as our nation's president, Obama continued to have his hair cut by the salon's owner Ishmael Coye so he could keep up with his favorite barber.

Today, visitors to the storied salon can sit beside the exact chair Barack Obama sat in while receiving his trims. Friendly service and sage advice are a given at this old-school-style barbershop that doubles as a makeshift shrine to the Chicago Bears, boxing legend Muhammad Ali, who also used to live in the neighborhood, and of course, hometown hero, Obama. The salon is a full-service shop that also offers manicures, pedicures, hot lather shaves, facials, massage therapy and shoe shines. Even bald men can count on a stellar service that will leave their head polished and protected. The $21 Obama Cut promises you'll leave the salon as dapper as the former president. Walk-ins are welcome, but your best bet is to call ahead for an appointment.

Unfortunately, visitors hoping to sit in the chair will be disappointed. In February 2009, R. S. Owens & Company, the Chicago-based manufacturer of trophies, including the Academy Awards, gifted the salon a Plexiglas case to protect this piece of presidential history.

Address Dorchester Commons Shopping Center, 5234 S Blackstone Avenue, Chicago, IL 60615, +1 (773) 493-6028, www.hydeparkhairsalon.com | **Getting there** Train to 55th-56th-57th St. (Metra Electric and South Shore Line) | **Hours** Daily 9am–8pm | **Tip** A simple rock with a metallic plate at 53rd Street and S Dorchester in Hyde Park marks the spot where former President Barack Obama first kissed his wife Michelle. This was once the site of a Baskin-Robbins ice cream shop, where the young couple enjoyed a moment sweeter than a sundae on their very first date back in the summer of 1989.

67_Ohio House Motel

Mid-century mod motel gem

The Ohio House Motel is reminiscent of Virginia Lee Burton's Caldecott Medal-winning children's book, *The Little House*, a poignant story of a sweet country cottage that is swallowed up by the city that expands upward around it. Like the little house, this retro motel still stands smack dab in the center of downtown Chicago, surrounded by tall skyscrapers.

The 50-room motel sprouted up on the corner of LaSalle and Ohio Streets in December 1960. As the years went by, the surrounding neighborhood first turned seedy and later became swanky. Older buildings were torn down to make way for the new high-rises. By the late 1990s, the motel's owner planned to demolish it and replace it with a larger hotel chain franchise. Thankfully, the plans never came to fruition, and the Ohio House Motel remains a tiny, independent, mid-century motor court in the midst of a bustling 21st century city.

The two-story motel features a funky diamond motif on its signage as well as the exterior of the buildings. A white concrete lace wall protects the motor court. Indeed, the Ohio House Motel is one of the only places in the city where you can still pull up your car and park right in front of your room, just as in decades past. A corner building with rough-faced stone walls still houses the motel's offices and a classic diner. The tall, triple diamond-shaped stainless steel sign, held up by a geometric metal grid, advertises the motel to motorists rambling down Ohio Street, into the heart of the city.

The Ohio House also features retro-style room rates – quite a bit less than many nearby hotels – and includes free roomside parking.

"Our guests are reminded of a bygone era, when the world was a more safe and secure place to live in," explains general manager Larry James. "Our excellent service and comfort reflects the higher level of service of the fifties and sixties."

Address 600 N La Salle Drive, Chicago, IL 60654, +1 (312) 943-6000, www.ohiohousemotel.com | Getting there Subway to Grand (Red Line) | Tip The motel's midcentury, in-house coffee shop traded drip coffee for cafe con leche and empanadas when it was taken over by the team behind the hip micro-chain Cafe Tola.

68_Old St. Patrick's Church

Cornerstone of Irish culture

Founded by faithful Irish immigrants on Easter Sunday, 1846, in a wooden building at Randolph Street and Desplaines Street, vibrant Old St. Patrick's Church is considered the cornerstone of Irish-American culture in Chicago. The present Romanesque-style church building, with its glorious Celtic Revival ornamentation, soaring octagonal spire, and yellow Cream City brick from Milwaukee set on a Lemont limestone base, was dedicated on Christmas Day, 1856, making it one of the few buildings to survive the Chicago Fire and the oldest standing church building in the city of Chicago. Celebrate mass here to connect with seven generations of parishioners, take part in one of the church's many neighborhood, volunteer outreach programs, or attend the summer block party, where chances are good that you will probably bump into your future bride or groom.

St. Patrick's been connecting faith, community, and the Irish culture in Chicago, which boasts the fourth-largest population of Irish Americans in the country, for close to 175 years. Upon arrival in Chicago, Irish immigrants would head straight to St. Pat's where they were welcomed with food, shelter, and the support of other parishioners who were already well on their way towards the American Dream.

The interior of the church, which many compare to sitting inside an Easter egg, was inspired by the Celtic art exhibit at the Columbian Exposition of 1893. Chicago artist Thomas O'Shaughnessy created the 15 magnificent, Art Nouveau stained-glass windows, each pane inspired by the Book of Kells and depicting a scene from the lives of the famous saints of Ireland. A towering statue of St. Patrick stands by the altar, welcoming his Irish family to Chicago.

In 1997, Oprah Winfrey deemed it one of the best places to meet your future spouse, and the event has led to 105 confirmed marriages.

Address 700 W Adams Street, Chicago, IL 60661, +1 (312) 648-1021 | Getting there Subway to Clinton (Blue Line) | Hours Tue–Sun 6:30am–1pm; Sun 6:30am–12:15pm & 4–9pm; closed to general public on Saturdays | Tip Docents are available to conduct guided tours of Old St. Pat's between 8am and 11am, Monday through Friday.

69 Optimo Hats

Bringing back bold elegance one hat at a time

Chicago was once a hat-wearing town, with new styles of classic men's hats hitting the streets every decade. Smart hats were *de rigueur* for the modern man, no matter his profession, social status, or stature. Then came John F. Kennedy, who rarely wore a hat of any kind during his presidency, setting off a trend that brings us to bare-headed today. Optimo Hats is on a mission to bring back bold, elegant statement hats to men in Chicago and beyond.

The walls and display windows of Optimo Hats are lined with the most beautiful men's hats you'll ever encounter. Straw hats are made from the highest quality hand-woven straw, imported from Ecuador, while the felt of the fedoras is crafted from wild animal furs, as opposed to cheaper wool alternatives. The bindings and ribbons are hand-stitched with the finest silk threads.

A retro circumference-measuring tool and a flange stand, used to flatten and shape the brim to each customer's taste, ensure the perfect custom fit. The hats here are offered in three sizes between conventional sizes, as well as in four oval head shapes, creating an individualized, air-cushioned fit. The sales staff will guide you towards that impossibly perfect-fitting hat, which should gently grip your head and yet be able to be easily tugged down a bit when the windy city lives up to its reputation. Prices match the time-consuming hat making process coupled with the finest materials; the most expensive hats run into the thousands. You might recognize Optimo hats in the movies *J. Edgar*, *Public Enemies*, and *Road to Perdition*.

Customers also have their pick from a wide range of fine vintage and modern hat ribbons from around the world. Once the ribbon is traditionally folded and sewn by hand using traditional millinery stitches to craft the bow and ensure no thread is visible, you'll know you're walking away with a museum-quality masterpiece that will bring a little more retro class and style to your modern-day life.

Address 51 W Jackson Boulevard, Chicago, IL 60604, +1 (312) 922-2999, www.optimo.com | Getting there Subway to Jackson (Blue Line) or Harold Washington Library-State/Van Buren (Brown, Orange, Pink, and Purple Line) | Hours Mon–Sat 10am–5pm | Tip See if you can spot the 31-foot-tall statue of the Roman goddess Ceres who keeps watch from the top of the nearby Chicago Board of Trade. Though it's normally closed to the public, the Chicago Board of Trade offers private tours by appointment (141 W Jackson Boulevard, +1 (312) 435-3590, www.cbot.com).

70_Oriental Institute

Unleash your inner Indiana Jones

Where else can you pet a 40-ton human-headed winged bull, stare into the eyes of King Tutankhamen, or try your hand at interpreting the many spells contained in a papyrus segment from a Ptolemaic period *Book of the Dead*? The University of Chicago's Oriental Institute has been digging up treasures from faraway lands since 1919, amassing a collection that offers a unique glimpse into ancient civilizations lost to the sands of time.

Many point to Professor James Henry Breasted, founder of the Oriental Institute with funds donated by John D. Rockefeller, Jr., as the inspiration behind Indiana Jones. But Breasted was no reckless treasure hunter; rather he was a committed field researcher with a knack for interpreting ancient writings, especially those from sources and structures that he feared may be lost forever. He even assisted Howard Carter in deciphering the seals from the Tomb of Tutankhamen.

Housed in an unusual Art Deco / Gothic building at the corner of 58th Street and University Avenue, the collection includes must-see oddities including an ear stella – a small tablet similar in size to an iPhone and believed to be a direct conduit to the Gods; a coffin containing a mummified lizard; and the mummy of forever-lovely Meresamun, a "Singer in the Interior of the Temple of Amun" at Karnak. The highlight of the collection is the enormous *lamassu*, a sculpture depicting a protective human-bull-bird spirit that once guarded the entrance to the throne room of King Sargon II. Viewed from the side, the creature appears to be walking; but when viewed from the front, it appears to be standing still.

Self-guided activities are available in both English and Spanish, including a popular treasure hunt. Don't forget to stop at the Suq (Arabic for market) on your way out, where you'll find a great array of jewelry, crafts, and gift items from the Near East.

Address The University of Chicago, 1155 E 58th Street, Chicago, IL 60637, +1 (773) 702-9520, www.oi.uchicago.edu | **Getting there** Train to 59th Street/University of Chicago (Metra Electric Line) | **Hours** Tue–Sun 10am–5pm (Wed until 8pm) | **Tip** Though now occupied by the Phi Gamma Delta frat, James Henry Breasted's Hyde Park home, designed to resemble the villa of Ariosto in Ferrara, Italy, features two ancient Egyptian-style serpents on either side of the front door (5615 S University Avenue).

71_Osaka Garden

Rising phoenix

Chicago's White City bloomed into being for the 1893 World's Columbian Exposition, dazzling visitors with its grand neoclassical buildings, surrounded by canals and ornate gardens designed by renowned landscape architect Frederick Law Olmsted.

But these opulent structures were not designed to last forever. The fancy façades were made not of marble, but of a cheap mixture of plaster, cement, and jute fiber, whitewashed with oil and lead paint. Of the over 200 buildings erected for the exposition, only two still stand. After the fair was over, Jackson Park, the expo's epicenter, was transformed into an interconnected system of serene lagoons surrounding the 15-acre Wooded Island.

Wooded Island was where fairgoers went to catch a breath of fresh air. At its northern end stood the *Ho-o-Den*, a.k.a. Phoenix Pavilion, a showcase of Japanese fine arts. At the southern end was the strolling garden, or *kyuushiki*, with its double pond, cascading waterfall, and stone pathways through the cherry blossom trees. Now known as the Osaka Garden and named for the long-standing Sister Cities relationship with the city of Osaka in Japan, the garden's blooming flowers offered welcome shade and respite to fairgoers and modern strollers today.

In the 1930s, more Japanese elements were added, including the scenic Moon Bridge and stone lanterns. Across the lagoon lies the last remaining structure of the 1893 fair, the Palace of Fine Arts, which is today's Museum of Science and Industry.

In 2014, the garden closed so that the U.S. Army Corps of Engineers could step in to restore the eroding lagoon shores, reset rocks, and replace invasive trees with 400,000 native plants. In 2016, Yoko Ono unveiled the lotus-inspired Sky Landing, her first permanent work of art in the Americas, as a gesture of peace, harmony and healing in the rebirthed garden.

Address 6401 S South Stony Island Avenue, Chicago, IL 60637, www.hydepark.org | **Getting there** Train to 63rd Street (Metra Electric Line) | **Hours** Daily 9am–5pm | **Tip** The "Golden Lady" sculpture, a one-third scale replica of Daniel Chester French's original Statue of the Republic, which was the centerpiece of the 1893 World's Columbian Exposition, stands in the area between the exposition's Electricity and Administration Buildings (both demolished after the exposition), now an intersection, where Richards Drive joins Hayes Drive (www.hydepark.org).

72_Outspoken at Sidetrack

Everyone has a story

Chicago's Boystown is home to highly active, visible, and vibrant LGBTQ communities. As the first officially recognized gay village in the country, this dynamic East Lakeview neighborhood, bordered by Lake Michigan on the east and Clark Street on the west, Irving Park Road to the north and Diversey Avenue to the south, is home to over 30 different gay and lesbian bars, nightclubs, and restaurants. If you want to find the beating heart of this community, you'll do so at Sidetrack, a huge Boystown hotspot that offers a monthly live storytelling show focused on the personal stories of LGBTQ-identified performers: Outspoken.

The stories told at Outspoken range from the side-splitting to the tear-jerking. Expect six storytellers from all walks of life, sharing stories that are not always gay-themed but always thought-provoking. Intimate and lively, this is a monthly event that aims to create a connection between the storytellers and the audience members, making for a wonderful opportunity to interact with the Boystown community in a fun and friendly atmosphere. Kim Hunt of Affinity Community Services, a social justice organization that focuses on health and wellness, leadership development, and community building among Chicago's LGBTQ youth, and Art Johnston, founder of Equality Illinois, serve as emcees. Each show promises to be unique, and the roster of featured storytellers changes each month. One reviewer calls Outspoken, "One of the best evenings you will spend in the midst of humanity."

Sidetrack, which lies at the heart of Boystown on the Halsted strip, spans more than eight storefronts and multiple levels, including an open-air courtyard and a lush rooftop deck. In addition to Outspoken, the bar hosts a variety of other community-minded fundraisers and events throughout the year. There is no cover fee, but you must be 21 and have a valid ID.

Address Sidetrack, 3349 N Halsted Street, Chicago, IL 60657, +1 (773) 477-9189, www.sidetrackchicago.com | Getting there Subway to Belmont (Red, Brown, and Purple Line) | Hours 1st Tue of every month; doors open 6pm; stories begin 7pm | Tip The city's annual Gay and Lesbian Pride Parade kicks off on the last Sunday of June with marching bands, grand floats, dance troupes, twirlers, celebrities and many political figures parading down Halsted and Broadway, the main streets of Boystown. Visit www.chicagopride.gopride.com for information and updates.

73_Oz Park

Follow the yellow brick road

In the 1890s, a certain L. Frank Baum, a reporter for the Chicago Evening Post, dreamed up a fantastical story: a cyclone whirls a young farm girl and her little dog up and away and into a land inhabited by merry Munchkins, winged monkeys, a wicked witch, and a charlatan ruler. Though the name Oz came from his file cabinet labeled "O-Z," many scholars of this American fairy tale believe that the mystical land was inspired by the glimmering "White City" that was the 1893 Chicago World's Fair.

Baum's beloved characters, who jumped from the printed page to the silver screen in 1939, live on in charming Oz Park. From the corner of Webster Avenue and Larabee Street, follow the yellow brick road towards the Emerald Garden, where you will be greeted by the Scarecrow. At the southeast corner, the bronze Cowardly Lion proudly displays his badge of courage. Dorothy and Toto watch over the children as they head towards the playground swings and slides. The Tin Man guards the northeast corner, proudly displaying his brand new, ticking heart. The statues were all created by John Kearney, a Chicago and Provincetown-based artist famous for his figurative sculptures made of found metal objects. He welded together old chrome car bumpers to bring Oz Park's Tin Man to life.

One of the park's major benefactors shares a first name with the Kansas girl who lost and then found herself in the Land of Oz: Dorothy Melamerson, a Chicago public school physical education teacher, who preferred to live a frugal life so that she could ultimately gift the children of her city this cherished, 13-plus-acre park. Melamerson also donated enough money to create the park's baseball fields and basketball, tennis, and volleyball courts, as well as the extensive youth sports initiative, a legacy that is reflected in the smiling faces of the many youngsters who joyfully claim this park as their own.

Address 2021 N Burling Street, Chicago, IL 60614, www.chicagoparkdistrict.com/parks | Getting there Subway to Armitage (Brown and Purple Line) | Hours Daily 6am–11pm | Tip Oz Park is one of many Chicago parks that show free outdoor movies as part of the Movies in the Park summer series. Bring a blanket and spread it on the grass, under the stars, for a truly unique movie-going experience. Visit www.chicagoparkdistrict.com/events/movies for the full summer schedule.

74_Palm Court at the Drake Hotel

Timeless tea

For nearly a century, savvy ladies have spent entire afternoons sipping tea beside a fountain in the Drake Hotel's gilded Palm Court. No one can pinpoint exactly why time stands still in this posh retreat as you enjoy your elegant afternoon tea. Maybe it is the enchanting ambiance amidst an array of potted palms, coupled with the pre-tea coupe of champagne. Perhaps it is the soft, flattering light emanating from the stained-glass ceiling and the lulling melodies of the live harpist. Queen Elizabeth, Princess Diana, and the Empress of Japan have all luxuriated in a spot of tea at the timeless Palm Court.

Every day afternoon tea is served between 1pm and 5pm at the Palm Court, located just off the hotel's main lobby. Seventeen tea selections created by Le Palais des Thés are on the menu, including the original Palm Court blend, all served in signature sterling silver teapots. Tiered platters of finger sandwiches, festive petit fours, English scones, and mini lemon poppyseed loaves are accompanied by fine preserves, lemon curd, and rich English Devon Cream.

The centerpiece of the Palm Court is the gorgeous marble fountain overflowing with flowers. Don't leave without making a wish, as the fountain is filled with coins that are donated to a local charity after a year's worth of accumulation.

Chicago's Drake Hotel has been welcoming visitors from its perch at the start of the Magnificent Mile since it was inaugurated on New Year's Eve in 1920. Designed with the palaces of High Renaissance Italy in mind, the hotel's 537 guest rooms and 74 suites have hosted important cultural and political figures from around the world. Several movies have been filmed under its roof, including *Time and Again*(1980), *The Blues Brothers*(1980), *Continental Divide*(1981), *Risky Business*(1983), and *My Best Friend's Wedding*(1997).

Address 140 E Walton Place, Chicago, IL 60611, +1 (312) 787-2200, www.thedrakehotel.com/dining/palm-court | **Getting there** Subway to Chicago (Red Line) | **Hours** Daily 1–5pm | **Tip** Post-tea, head to the bar at the Drake's Coq d'Or for bookbinder soup (a Drake classic) and executive martinis.

75_Palmer Mausoleum

Beware of wandering ghosts

Potter Palmer and his stunning wife Bertha were the toast of Gilded Age Chicago. Potter is best known for developing State Street, and in particular for his enormous Palmer House Hotel, a wedding gift that literally went up in flames. He built the elegant hotel, the first of its kind in Chicago, in honor of his beautiful new wife, Bertha. An unlucky thirteen days after his hotel opened on September 26, 1871, it burned down to the ground in the Great Chicago Fire.

But not even the Great Chicago Fire could derail the Palmers' dreams. Potter secured a $1.7 million signature loan and rebuilt his hotel and his fortune. Bertha, who Potter so famously spoiled with diamonds and pearls, went to become the queen of Chicago high society, a patron of Impressionist artists and the inventor of the brownie.

While the Palmers lived in a Gold Coast Gothic-style castle, today they rest eternally within the two large granite sarcophagi at ghostly Graceland Cemetery. Three generations of their descendants lie beside them in this, the grandest tomb of Graceland. It was designed by the firm of McKim, Mead & White to resemble a Greek temple. When Mrs. Palmer died in Florida in 1918, she was transported here in a coffin covered in a blanket of orchids. The inverted torches on the sides of their sarcophagi symbolize death.

The Victorian Graceland Cemetery is considered to be one of the most paranormally active sites in Chicago, so beware of wandering ghosts. It is the final resting place of many of Chicago's most illustrious early citizens. Architect Louis Sullivan, who is also buried here, designed the ornate tomb of lumber baron Henry Harrison Getty. An Egyptian-style granite pyramid serves as the mausoleum for the family of beer brewer Peter Schoenhofen. Industrialist George Pullman rests here in a steel-and-concrete reinforced vault, to prevent his body from being exhumed by angry labor activists.

Address 4001 N Clark Street, Chicago, IL 60613, +1 (773) 525-1105, www.gracelandcemetery.org | Getting there Subway to Sheridan (Red Line) | Hours Mon–Fri 8am–6pm; Sat 10am–3pm; check website for the fall & winter opening hours | Tip A spooky statue by famous American sculptor Lorado Taft marks the grave of early Chicago pioneer Dexter Graves (1789-1844). The mysterious, bronze hooded man was officially named *Eternal Silence*. It is more commonly referred to as the Statue of Death. Legend has it that if you look into the statue's black eyes, you will see your own death unfold.

76 Palmisano Park

From coral reef to quarry to peaceful city oasis

Palmisano Park knows a thing or two about adapting to the changing tides of time. Over the centuries, it has transformed from a coral reef to a quarry, to landfill, and finally to the beautiful 27-acre park that it is today. Located in the heart of Bridgeport, this peaceful park, with its fishing pond, wetlands, quarry walls, and trailways, is one of Chicago's most dynamic green spaces.

Once upon a time – 400 million years ago to be exact – this green escape from the city was part of a massive coral reef in the warm, shallow seas that covered what is now Chicago. As the Silurian Age faded into history, Dolomite limestone and fossils formed as curious ancient souvenirs. Later, in the late 1830s, when early entrepreneurs turned the site into a quarry, that same limestone was mined and used to build railroad embankments, bridges, tunnels, lake retaining walls, homes, foundations, and façades throughout Chicago. The quarry continued operating until 1970, its excavated hole having reached 380 feet below street level, when it was turned into a landfill for clean construction debris.

In 1999, the city decided to transform the park into much-need green space, and in 2009, Palmisano Park was inaugurated. It has been hailed as one of the best places to enjoy spending time outdoors, no matter the season.

Walk along over 1.7 miles of paths, where you are sure to find signs of Palmisano Park's past, such as the catch and release fishing pond situated 40 feet below street level which retains the original walls of the old quarry. Reclaimed wood found in the quarry was used to create the walkways. Old rocks from the quarry days dot the landscape. Climb the hill, which rises 33 feet above street level, to see the quarry's limestone legacy, a stunning view of the city built with the remains of an ancient reef mined from this now verdant corner of Bridgeport.

Address 2700 S Halsted Street, Chicago, IL 60608, +1 (312) 747-6497, www.chicagoparkdistrict.com/parks | Getting there Subway to Halsted (Orange Line) | Hours Daily 6am–11pm | Tip You can find a free self-guided audio tour of Palmisano Park, created by the Chicago Park District online. The tour includes a map with stopping points that correspond with the audio tracks. If you visit each place and listen to the tracks, your walking tour will take approximately 40 minutes (www.chicagoparkdistrict.com/about-us/audio-tours/palmisano-park).

77__Parrot Cage Restaurant

A+ brunch at the country club for everyone

In a grand Mediterranean Revival clubhouse, situated between an idyllic stretch of beachfront and the lush greenery of a golf course, ladies who lunch, dressed to the nines, sip champagne as they take in the panoramic view of Lake Michigan. It is a scene straight out of *The Great Gatsby*, and it takes place every weekend at the Parrot Cage, a gem of a restaurant in the grandiose South Shore Cultural Center. The staff members go above and beyond and are always eager to please even the most discerning diners: that's because the entire team that runs the Parrot Cage, from the wait staff to the cooks in the kitchen, are students-in-training at the Washburne Culinary Institute, one of the oldest culinary schools in the nation.

At one time, this building was a Protestant-only country club that lacked the diversity that makes it the rich, artistic hub that it is today. By 1975, the property, complete with a golf course, tennis courts, a bowling green, stables, theater, and a private beach, was sold to the Chicago Park District.

Today the South Shore Cultural Center houses the School of the Arts, which offers community dance, music, and art classes. The golf course, beach, and gardens are still open to the public, while the horse stables are currently used by the Chicago Police Department's Mounted Unit.

The Parrot Cage Restaurant, which offers modern American cuisine at ultra-affordable prices, gives culinary students the chance to hone their skills. Thanks to an A+ in enthusiasm, creativity, and exceptional culinary training, the restaurant has even earned the industry's prestigious Zagat rating of "excellent or better" for three consecutive years, and the Sunday brunch has repeatedly earned the OpenTable Diners' Top Choice award. Former President and First Lady Barack and Michelle Obama hosted their wedding reception at the South Shore Cultural Center in 1992.

Address 7059 S South Shore Drive, Chicago, IL 60649, +1 (773) 602-5333, www.washburneculinary.com/facilities/the-parrot-cage | Getting there Train to South Shore (Metra Electric Line) | Hours Thu–Sat 5–9pm; Sun 11am–3pm | Tip Rainbow Beach, a short walk along the lakefront from the Parrot Cage, is one of the best and biggest stretches of beach in Chicago, with a breathtaking view of the city skyline to boot. It was also the site of the 1961 "Freedom Wade-In," when an interracial coalition of demonstrators stood up to the longstanding hostility from lifeguards and white bathers, seeking to heighten public awareness and challenge segregation in Chicago (3111 E 77th Street, www.chicagoparkdistrict.com/parks).

78 Pickwick Alley

Passageway to Old Chicago

It is easy to miss Pickwick Lane unless you know it is there. Though it is located in the heart of the bustling Loop at 22 E Jackson Boulevard, this nine-foot-wide passageway, dead-ended by a three-story building, might be short in length, but it is long in history. Step onto its cobblestones and travel back in time to the Chicago of days gone by.

The city of Chicago grew up around that small building, still known as the Pickwick Stable, which is actually 19 feet wide, and 19 feet deep. Over 150 years ago, this lane led to an actual stable that was destroyed in the Great Chicago Fire. After the fire, grocer and flour merchant Henry Horner and his wife Fannie Abson purchased the lot, where they built the current two-story building, transforming the space into Colonel Abson's Chop House, a favorite eating establishment for Chicago's biggest bon vivants, especially the post-theatre crowd. The Absons later added the building's third floor and made it their home. After the chop house closed in 1900, a number of restaurants came and went in this space, including the Red Path Inn, Robinson's, Pickwick Cafe and 22 East. In the 1970s, the building was almost torn down, but thankfully this little corner of Old Chicago survived.

A small coffee shop with a few seats in the alley now thrives in what was once nothing more than a dead end and a horse stable. Some call it "an urban leftover," as it has remained as it was for decades while the area around it filled with new skyscrapers. The two buildings that flank the lane are the 16-story Gibbons Building and the 19-story landmarked Steger Building, which was originally home to a piano company. At night, with the tiny lights strung overhead, it is not difficult to imagine the comings and goings in Pickwick Lane and the days when horses made up most of Chicago's traffic.

Address 22 E Jackson Boulevard, Chicago, IL 60604 | Getting there Subway to Adams/Wabash (Brown, Orange, Purple, Green, and Pink Line) | Tip Steps away from Pickwick Alley, at Jackson Boulevard and Michigan Avenue, was the original starting point of the fabled Route 66, America's Main Street.

79_Pilsen Murals

Redefining a neighborhood

The murals that adorn just about every space in the Pilsen neighborhood reflect the residents' shared joys, sorrows, political concerns, memories, and Latino culture. What started as a Chicago Urban Art Society initiative, to drive out gang graffiti and brighten this corner of the city, has turned into a thought-provoking art gallery, sharing the stories of the residents via art and transforming the neighborhood into a creative hub.

Artist Francisco Mendoza was commissioned in 1993 to redefine the gateway to Pilsen. Together with a team of 20 young students, he created *Las Mujeres*(located on the exterior of the station on the east side of the entrance), a mosaic that celebrates the bold and beautiful women of Mexico, past and present. In 1998, Mendoza gathered a group of teens once again and packed the entire station with art – every solid surface is covered with a colorful mural expressing the rich Mexican heritage of Pilsen's residents.

At 1401 W 18th Street, the two-story *Declaration of Immigration*, created by artist Salvador Jimenez and a group of young students, poignantly reminds viewers that we are a city and a nation of immigrants. Pilsen has historically been a first-stop neighborhood for immigrants, having first welcomed immigrants from Bohemia and later from Mexico.

The mural *Gulliver En El País De Las Maravillas* (1900 W Cullerton Street) covers the studio home of its artist, Hector Duarte. Inspired by *Gulliver's Travels*, it depicts Gulliver not as a traveler in a new land, but as a Mexican immigrant struggling to break free from a barbed wire fence. *Increíbles Las Cosas Q' Se Ven*by Jeff Zimmerman pays homage to the sacrifices of past generations for the benefit of the next, and depicts migrants crossing a river, the faces of blue collar workers, and finally, two proud Mexican-American graduates with a bold and true reminder: "Si, se puede" – Yes, you can.

Getting there Subway to 18th (Pink Line) | Tip Cap off your tour of Pilsen with a visit to the Nuestras Historias exhibit at the National Museum of Mexican Art. This dynamic permanent exhibit highlights the Mexican identity as seen through art from past to present (852 W 19th Street, www.nationalmuseumofmexicanart.org).

80 Poetry Foundation

The power of poetry

Ruth Lilly, heiress to the Lilly family pharmaceutical fortune, loved reading and writing poetry. For years she submitted her poems to the renowned *Poetry* magazine, unsuccessfully. Nevertheless, Lilly did not let her rejection undermine her support of the famed magazine. In 2002, she donated $100 million to *Poetry*. Part of her bequest was used to build a new home for the Poetry Foundation, marking the first space in Chicago dedicated solely to the art of poetry.

Founded in Chicago in 1912, *Poetry* is one of the world's leading monthly poetry journals in the English-speaking world, having featured the works of Gwendolyn Brooks, T. S. Eliot, Robert Frost, Ezra Pound, Carl Sandburg, Dylan Thomas, and William Carlos Williams. The Poetry Foundation's new River North headquarters, designed by John Ronan Architects, opened in 2011 and houses a public library, gallery, and garden, as well as office space for the Poetry Foundation and magazine.

When Harriet Monroe founded *Poetry* magazine, she began with an image: the Open Door. "May the great poet we are looking for never find it shut, or half-shut, against his ample genius!" Following Monroe's proclamation, to enter the Poetry Foundation, you walk through an opening in the black screen wall rather than any grand, gilded doors. You can also find Harriet Monroe, in a Pointillist rendering, on the wall next to the performance space door.

Inside, an elevated courtyard features a mirrored tribute to Lilly. The Foundation's extensive library, the Midwest's only library dedicated exclusively to poetry, holds over 30,000 volumes and features private listening booths where visitors can listen to audio and video poetry recordings. While you can always stop in for a moment of poetry reading and repose, the Poetry Foundation hosts almost daily readings, workshops, and performances, for poets and lovers of poetry alike.

Address 61 W Superior Street, Chicago, IL 60654, +1 (312) 787-7070, www.poetryfoundation.org | Getting there Subway to Chicago (Red Line) | Hours Mon–Fri 11am–4pm | Tip The Poetry Foundation's POETRY mobile app, available on iTunes and Google Play, gives poetry lovers access to hundreds of poems by classic and contemporary poets. Give your phone a shake to discover new poems to fit any mood.

81_Pothole Art

Bumps in the road

It takes a truckload of ingenuity to transform a troubling eyesore into a work of art. Chicago artist Jim Bachor has gone above and beyond. He has taken on the challenge of patching up Chicago's most dastardly potholes and makes mosaics out of them, thus providing a community service for both the city's streets and its artful spirit. His 30-plus pothole art masterpieces are reminders of the power of creativity to transform even the worst lemons into lemonade, making light of the bumps in the road of life by turning them into places of beauty and creativity.

Chicago's wide range of high and low temperatures makes for plenty of potholes. The period from December through April is considered peak pothole season as the snow and cold cause dangerous cavities to erupt inwards on streets across the city. City road crews fixed potholes in their thousands around the city last year, even going so far as to set up a Pothole Tracker that maps potholes patched by the Department of Transportation in the previous seven days, based on corresponding 311 city service delivery requests. But it seems that as soon as one pit is patched up seemingly for good, another one appears steps away, much to the dismay of Chicago drivers.

Bachor's self-proclaimed pothole revitalization initiative dates back to 2013, when he patched up a pothole in front of his home in the Mayfair neighborhood. He has transformed potholes into beautiful and quirky mosaics, modern versions of Roman mosaic floors. You'll come across ice cream cones, creamsicles, daffodils, blue birds. He has also patched potholes with Burberry plaid, red and green Gucci stripes, and Louis Vuitton logos, as well as helpful messages that say both "Pothole" and "This Is Not a Pothole."

An interactive map at www.bachor.com details the exact locations, but it's best to be caught unaware by these ever-evolving installations.

Address See www.bachor.com for an interactive map of Bachor's playful pothole installations. | Tip Chicago's streets are arranged in an iconic grid system, the epicenter of which is the intersection of State and Madison Streets, in the heart of the Loop. Each street is prefaced with "East" or "West," depending on whether they fall east or west of State Street; "North" and "South" denote whether streets fall north or south of Madison Street. Address numbers increase or decrease depending on their distance in miles from the State and Madison epicenter, with odd numbers sticking to the south and east sides of streets, and even numbers on the north and west sides.

82_The Rainbo Club

Stare into the shot glass's false bottom

In Nelson Algren's 1949 classic movie *The Man with the Golden Arm*, Frankie Majcinek, a veteran of World War II, struggles to make ends meet while fighting a growing addiction to drugs and alcohol – "For way down there, in a shot glass's false bottom, everything was bound to turn out fine after all." Much of the story takes place during the immediate postwar period along Division Street and Milwaukee Avenue, Chicago's old Polish Downtown. The Rainbo Club, one of Algren's favorite local haunts, is the inspiration for the fictional Tug & Maul bar, where Majcinek tried his best to drink his cares away: "The Tug & Maul, this winter noon, looked much as it had that Easter Dawn. Frost had gathered on the windows and by night there would be neon rainbows in the snow."

Algren lived on the third floor of a three-story walkup, walking distance from the Rainbo Club at 1958 W Evergreen Avenue. Look for the plaque that commemorates his time spent in the apartment.

Dive bar *par excellence*, the Rainbo Club has undergone several incarnations in its long history. It has been a bar within a drugstore, a burlesque bar, a speakeasy, and a Polka-dancing watering hole, since it first opened in 1936. Despite its various transformations, not much has changed inside. It is easy to imagine burlesque dancers shimmying atop the white clam-like Art Deco stage behind the bar. Patrons still belly up to the bar or sink into the red vinyl seats, still trying their best to wash down their worries with shots, much like Frankie Majcinek in the movie and Nelson Algren, who was a regular, did in the forties. Liz Phair's 1993 album *Exile in Guyville* was inspired by the Rainbo Club, with its regular patrons who, despite the passage of time, have always fitted the down-and-out artist bill, and the neighborhood that grew up around it; the album's cover photo was shot in the bar's photo booth.

Address 1150 N Damen Avenue, Chicago, IL 60622, +1 (773) 489-5999 | **Getting there** Subway to Division (Blue Line) | **Hours** Daily 4pm–2am (Sat open until 3am) | **Tip** At the center of Chicago's "Polish Triangle," a triangular intersection of Ashland Avenue, Milwaukee Avenue, and Division Street, lies a black cast-iron fountain, dedicated to Nelson Algren in 1998. The inscription on the fountain's base, "For the masses who do the city's labor also keep the city's heart," is from Algren's 1951 essay "Chicago: City on the Make."

83 Red Square Spa

Steam your cares away

If you're looking to steam out all the toxic elements from your life, or if you'd just love to indulge in a few vodka shots, borscht, and blini following a deep tissue massage, make a beeline to Red Square Spa, a modern, Russian-style spa housed in a historic Chicago bathhouse.

Because of inadequate indoor plumbing in most homes, it wasn't until the early 1900s that Chicagoans began to bathe with regularity. Thanks to a push for public bathhouses, led by the Municipal Order League and three women physicians, city officials established 21 small and utilitarian public bathhouses in poor and immigrant neighborhoods between 1894 and 1918. One of these bathhouses was the Division Street Russian and Turkish Baths, which opened in 1906 and offered separate bathing facilities for men and women. In 2013, it was transformed into today's Red Square Spa. Check out the original brick ovens in both the men's and women's *banya*, or hot rooms. If you can manage to open the door without burning your hands, you will spot giant granite boulders inside, which are heated to 800 degrees F every night with gas jets, maintaining their heat throughout the following day.

Give the traditional *platza* spa treatment a try. You will be lightly whipped with birch, eucalyptus, or oak branches by an esthetician as you lie flat on a wooden bench in the *banya*. Your eyes will be covered with a cool facecloth, so you will be even more surprised when the esthetician dumps icy cold water on your body. While it might not prove to be the most relaxing spa treatment you will ever experience, it will undoubtedly improve your circulation temporarily and open up your pores – both essentials if you are looking to detox.

Autographed photos of celebrity visitors line the first-floor hallway, and if you're lucky you might run into a famous person or two dressed to the nines in a bathrobe.

Address 1914 W Division Street, Chicago, IL 60622, +1 (773) 227-2284, www.redsquarechicago.com | Getting there Subway to Division (Blue Line) | Hours Mon–Fri 10am–11pm; Sat & Sun 7–12am | Tip Red Square Spa's first-floor restaurant and bar resembles an elegant, 19th-century luxury train dining car and features all your Russian favorites. While it's not necessarily low-calorie spa cuisine, you're welcome to dine in your waist-friendly spa robe.

84_Robinson Woods

Where the ghosts are

Mysterious shadows, strange sounds, glowing orbs, and even an ectoplasmic mist have all allegedly been caught red-handed on camera in the ancient Native American burial ground hidden in the woods just off bustling Lawrence Avenue. If you are looking to scare your pants off at perhaps Chicago's most paranormal place, grab a flashlight and hike into Robinson Woods in the dead of night ... if you dare.

Chee-Chee-Pin-Quay, a.k.a. Alexander Robinson, was the fur-dealing son of a Scottish trader and a Chippewa woman. When Fort Dearborn was attacked by the Potawatomi in August 1812, Robinson helped broker the release of the fort's captain and some of the early Chicago settlers who had been held captive after the battle. About half of today's 265-acre Robinson Wood was gifted to Robinson in gratitude. His descendants continued to live in a home that once stood here until 1955, when it burned to the ground. A large granite memorial marks the burial site of both Robinson and his French wife Catherine Chevalier, as well as many of their 14 children and grandchildren. When the city of Chicago annexed the land during construction of O'Hare Airport, city officials promised Robinson's sole living descendant that he too could be buried here among his ancestors. When he died, however, the city broke its promise, which, according to legend, set off the paranormal activity that carries on to this day.

Visitors often report hearing the sound of beating tribal drums, and smelling freshly-cut flowers even when the woods are covered with snow. Follow the unmarked footpath from the small parking lot, as it leads to some old fencing and a lane, marking the site of the Robinson homestead. Most paranormal activity seems to come from the left side of the Robinson Family Monument. In addition to ghosts, the riverside preserve is also home to deer, beavers, turtles, and mallards.

Address W Lawrence Avenue at the Des Plaines River, www.fpdcc.com/robinson-woods | Getting there Subway to Rosemont (Blue Line) then Pace bus 301, 303, 308, and 332 to River/Lawrence | Tip For the main entrance to Robinson Woods, turn east/left on Lawrence Avenue; the parking area is on the south side of the street. To access the Robinson family burial grounds, continue east on Lawrence and turn north/left on E River Road. The small pull out is on the west side of the road.

85_Rosa's Lounge

Hidden home of the blues

Rosa's Lounge is one of the few remaining off-the-radar Chicago blues clubs in the city. *Rolling Stone* magazine called it "a blues mecca for true believers," and indeed a visit to this old-school haven will make both novice and long-established blues fans feel at home. Hidden in the North Side neighborhood of Logan Square, this hidden gem keeps the blues rolling on a high note even as more and more blues-centered clubs call it a night.

Owner Tony Mangiullo felt the blues in his bones ever since he was a little boy living across the ocean, in Milan, Italy. After a chance backstage encounter with iconic vocalist and harmonica player Junior Wells, Manguillo decided to follow his heart and leave la bell'Italia for the home of urban blues. Inspired by his time spent in now-shuttered South Side blues clubs, including the legendary Theresa's Lounge, Manguillo opened Rosa's Lounge, named after his dear mamma who followed him to Chicago a year later, in 1984.

Nightly acts at Rosa's Lounge cover the entire spectrum of styles, with both longtime legends like David Honeyboy Edwards, Homesick James, and Pinetop Perkins to new-era greats including Billy Branch, Melvin Taylor, and Sugar Blue. Their photos line the walls, along with a photo of Barack Obama, a fundraising regular during his pre-presidential years in Chicago.

Considering that the lounge has played host to musical legends, it is a low key and intimate venue, with a long bar and just a few cocktail-sized tables for two scattered around a small stage, where all the magic happens each night. Get comfy in one of the tall vinyl bar seats and soak in the sounds. If you're lucky, Mamma Rosa herself, who still tends bar on occasion, will sling your drink. Try the house specialty, *pasta nonna*, or baked pasta with eggplant, just one more reason why Rosa's Lounge is known as Chicago's friendliest blues lounge.

Address 3420 W Armitage Avenue, Chicago, IL 60647, +1 (773) 342-0452, www.rosaslounge.com | **Getting there** Subway to California (Blue Line) | **Hours** Tue–Fri 8pm–2am; Sat 8pm–3am | **Tip** Craving the blues but can't make it out to the Windy City to catch an act at Rosa's? Check out the lounge's livestream at www.gigity.tv/rosaslounge.

86_School of Folk Music

"We wanted to make music accessible to everyone."

Win Strake was performing a three-week gig at the Gate of Horn, a famous, long-gone folk music club at Chicago and Dearborn, when he befriended multi-instrumentalist Frank Hamilton, a fellow young, struggling folk musician. The duo befriended Dawn Greening, an Oak Park housewife and hardcore folk music fan, who kindly offered up her dining room as a place where Hamilton could make a few bucks teaching his trade to eager young artists. Strake soon found himself attending one of Hamilton's dining room classes, and was so intrigued by new methods and music that he proposed opening a folk music school. Together the pair developed a new music teaching method that focused on listening, watching, trial and error, and playing by ear. Some of the school's early teachers included Chicago blues guitarist Big Bill Broonzy, banjo players Fleming Brown and Stu Ramsey, and Brazilian singer-guitarist Valucha deCastro.

If you pass by the Old Town School of Folk Music on Lincoln Avenue today you'll hear music of all genres – rock, bluegrass, jazz, blues, country, and of course, folk – streaming from the school into the surrounding streets. Step into the concert hall, and you'll likely find a world-class musician onstage. Peek into a classroom, and you might see a group guitar lesson, or a children's movement workshop in action. Over 7,000 students attend classes here on any given week.

One of the best ways to experience the vibrant community that is the Old Town School of Folk Music is to hit one of the weekly jam sessions. Pick a genre and bring your voice or your instrument. You don't need to be a student, and you don't need to be a star; you just need to be willing to make new music with new friends. If you love folk music, the Great Americana Songbook Jam takes place every Wednesday from noon to 2pm; the Folk, Rock and Roots Jam rocks out every Thursday from 7pm to 10pm.

Address 4544 N Lincoln Avenue, Chicago, IL 60625, +1 (773) 728-6000, www.oldtownschool.org | **Getting there** Subway to Western (Brown Line) | **Hours** Mon–Thu 9am–10pm; Fri–Sun 9am until 1 hr past the day's final show time | **Tip** The in-house Music Store offers new and used instruments for sale and rent; restrings with a next-day turn around and tuning; and "a wide range of opinions on most musical topics, available for free every day."

87_School of Shoemaking

Finding the sole of the city

In a former factory loft lined with exposed brick and wooden beams, a cobbler with over 40 years of experience carefully hand stitches an insole. The rich, warm smell of smooth leather permeates the air. Steel cutters, iron pliers, brass-handle awls, scissors, punches, and hammers hang from the walls and wait patiently on large wood work tables. It is a scene straight out of "The Elves and the Shoemaker." But this busy cobbler is no little old man: she's Sara McIntosh, founder of the Chicago School of Shoemaking & Leather Arts. And her elves-in-training are men and women from across the city, all eager to discover the long-lost craft of handmade shoes.

Chicago School of Shoemaking & Leather Arts is one of the few remaining schools in the world that teaches the art of shoemaking. Take one class at this school, and you'll leave with a truly unique pair of sandals, moccasins, or boots that are comfortable, sustainable, and promise to last for years. Small class sizes – no more than four students per class – and personalized instruction mean that budding cobblers will learn everything they need to craft high-quality shoes within the session timeframe, approximately 18 hours of class time. The school provides the patterns, midsoles, and soles based on your shoe size. You'll cut out the leather, prepare the materials, and stitch the leather uppers to the midsoles, glue those to the soles and then form the upper to the shape and size of your feet. After a few finishing details, you will proudly walk away in a pair of one-of-a-kind kicks.

"Our goal is to empower all people to enjoy a satisfying and liberating experience around creating footwear and leather work," declares the literature for this old-school school. "Buy a pair of shoes and you cover your feet for a year or two. Learn how to make shoes, and you can shoe yourself, family and friends for a lifetime."

Address 3717 N Ravenswood Avenue, Chicago, IL 60613, +1 (773) 334-2248, www.chicagoschoolofshoemaking.com | **Getting there** Subway to Addison (Brown and Purple Line) | **Hours** See website for class schedule | **Tip** At nearby Zan Atelier, tailor extraordinaire Nazia Zamani will work with you to design, create and customize clothing. If you're looking for the dress that you literally dreamed of, Zamani can bring it to life (1625 W Montrose Avenue, +1 (773) 348-8666, www.zanatelier.com).

88_Secret Mobster Vault

Home of the henchman

As one of Al Capone's top henchmen, Frank "The Enforcer" Nitti was in charge of the mob's "muscle" operations. He ran Al Capone's liquor smuggling and distribution operation, importing whisky from Canada and selling it through a network of speakeasies. He was one of Capone's most trusted bodyguards, and when Capone was arrested in 1929, he named Nitti as a member of a triumvirate that ran the mob during his stint in Philadelphia's Eastern State Penitentiary. Under Nitti's direction, the Chicago Outfit branched out from prostitution and gambling to control of labor unions and business extortion.

Nitti maintained a hideout at 33 W Kinzie Street, the Dutch Renaissance Revival-style former headquarters of the Chicago Varnish Company, built in 1895 and designed by Henry Ives Cobb. Under the guise of a cheese company, Nitti kept an apartment on the fourth floor from early 1939 until his death. From his window here, he could keep an eye on the nearby courthouse building; the basement was connected to the city's tunnel network, which allowed him to make a quick, covert escape.

In 1943, Nitti and other member of the Outfit were indicted for extorting the Hollywood film industry. Dreading the thought of incarceration – Nitti was claustrophobic – he sent his wife off to Our Lady of Sorrows church to pray for him. He began drinking heavily, loaded a .32 caliber revolver, walked to a local railroad yard, and shot himself in the head.

Today Harry Caray's Steak House occupies the building, but you can still sneak into Nitti's vault, which contains a remarkable collection of memorabilia, including a phonebook containing contact information for several reputed Chicago gangsters from the thirties and forties, a three-door safe from the early 1900s, and numerous original newspaper articles and photographs documenting the exploits of Nitti and his gang during the Capone era.

Address Harry Caray's, 33 W Kinzie Street, Chicago, IL 60654, +1 (312) 828-0962, www.harrycarays.com | **Getting there** Subway to Grand (Red Line) | **Hours** Mon–Thu 11:30am–10:30pm; Fri & Sat 11:30am–11pm; Sun 11:30am–10pm | **Tip** The Vault, accessible through Harry's Bar, can be viewed by guests at no cost during regular restaurant hours. Be sure to check out the other memorabilia showcasing the history of the Cubs and famed sportscaster Harry Caray's legacy (including a pair of Caray's iconic, oversized glasses) located throughout the restaurant and bar.

89_Showmen's Rest

Where the circus comes to rest

In the wee hours of June 22, 1918, engineer Alonzo Sargent's locomotive was pulling 20 empty Pullman cars when he fell asleep at the controls, ramming his empty Michigan Central Railroad troop train into a slower circus train, packed with performers, on the same tracks. Eighty-six circus members died from the impact, while another 127 were injured, when Sargent's train plowed into the caboose and four rear wooden sleeping cars of the circus train. Five days after the wreck, the many clowns, acrobats, aerialists, stuntmen, and strongmen were laid to rest in a mass grave that was dug out of a 750-plot section of Woodlawn Cemetery, that had coincidentally been recently purchased by the Showmen's League of America.

The headstones here bring the train tragedy to life. Some are inscribed with showbiz names – Baldy, Smiley; others indicate the deceased's role in the circus, such as "horse driver"; others are marked "Unidentified Male" or "Unidentified Female" – indicative of both the horrific collision and the circus lifestyle that often picked up new troupe members along the tracks to the next performance. The more famous showstoppers buried here include trapeze artist Jennie Ward Todd of the Flying Wards; strongmen Arthur Dieckx and Max Nietzborn of Great Dieckx Brothers fame; and the McDhu Sisters, noted aerialists and elephant wranglers. Five granite elephants, their trunks lowered in tribute, were added in the years that followed the tragedy, leading to rumors of ghostly circus animals wandering the graveyard at night, but the elephants that did die in the train crash were too heavy to move, and were buried beside the tracks.

Sargent was charged with manslaughter for falling asleep on the job, and the accident led to regulations mandating sleep for tired train crews. Showmen's Rest is still used today to inter deceased circus performers.

Address 7750 W Cermak Road, Forest Park, IL 60130, +1 (708) 442-8500, www.dignitymemorial.com/woodlawn-funeral-home-chicago | Getting there Subway to 54th/Cermak (Pink Line) then Pace bus 322 to Cermak/Burr Oak | Hours Daily 8am–6pm | Tip Every August, circus artists from across the world perform for the public at Showmen's Rest in an event billed as "a loving and festive remembrance of circus artists past" (www.performforthelove.com/showmensrest).

90_Signature Lounge Loo

(Rest)room with a view

So rarely do trips to the restroom reward one with fond memories, but slip away to the ladies' room at the Signature Cocktail Lounge and you'll be captivated. With the view, that is. Located on the 96th floor of the iconic John Hancock building, the restroom bestows a bathroom experience like no other, thanks to the stunning floor-to-ceiling windows that offer a bird's-eye view over the city. On a clear day, you can reapply your lipstick or powder your nose while taking in a vista that spans four states, with a visibility of up to four miles. Take your time because the views are breathtaking, particularly on a clear night.

When the 100-story, 1,128-foot-tall John Hancock Center was inaugurated in 1968, it was the second tallest building in the world. Today it remains the fourth tallest building in the city of Chicago and the eighth tallest building in the world. Known for its distinctive X-braced exterior, the building was designed by Bruce Graham and structural engineer Fazlur Khan, and constructed under the supervision of Chicago-based Skidmore, Owings and Merrill.

The Hancock Center's elevators are among the fastest in the world, and it takes just 40 seconds for guests to be whisked up from the ground floor to the 96th-floor cocktail lounge. While many engagements have been announced and anniversaries celebrated at the 95th-floor restaurant, The Signature Room, any occasion is a good occasion to enjoy cocktails at the "top of the 'cock." You'll want to sip one of the lounge's house-invented cocktails, the Gold Coast (Beefeater gin, Aperol and fresh lemon sour) or Signature Room Punch (Myer's Rum, Cruzan, fresh lime sour, grenadine, pineapple and orange juice).

If you suffer from vertigo, beware: on windy days, the building seriously sways – sometimes up to eight inches! – making a trip to the lounge's ladies room even more adventuresome.

Address John Hancock Center, 875 N Michigan Avenue, 96th floor, Chicago, IL 60611, +1 (312) 787-9596, www.signatureroom.com/lounge | Getting there Subway to Chicago (Red Line) | Hours Sun–Thu 11–12:30am; Fri & Sat 11–1:30am | Tip On the 94th floor of the John Hancock Center, brave guests can lean outward from 10 to 30 degrees on the Tilt, a set of eight movable, enclosed bays that offer a gripping downward look upon the city streets below.

91_Sky Chapel

Worshipping in the clouds

Reaching 568 feet into the air, the Sky Chapel is the world's tallest church. Aptly located in the metropolis that birthed the skyscraper, this church in the clouds is home to the congregation of the First United Methodist Church of Chicago, one of the city's earliest parishes.

An elevator whisks worshippers up directly to the chapel, which is tucked under the base of the skyscraping steeple. Sixteen stained-glass windows envelop congregants here, one of which memorializes the church's original riverside cabin. At its center, an illuminated altar depicts Jesus, carved in wood, as he weeps over Chicago and its people, who are still unaware of "the things that make for peace." It is easy to keep time here, despite the timeless ambiance: every 15 minutes digital church bells ring from speakers attached to the building. This is as close to the heavens as you'll get in Chicago.

The famed local architectural firm Holabird & Roche designed the neo-Gothic Chicago Temple building, which is constructed on a steel frame faced with limestone. The skytop chapel, once the building's bell tower, was a 1952 gift from the Walgreen family (of the eponymous drugstore chain). The space seats just 30, making it a popular site for small weddings. The chapel is both intimate and awe-inspiring, thanks to its bird's-eye view of the city from the patio.

The congregation, founded in 1831, established a church of their very own on the north bank of the Chicago River in 1834. From their first house of worship, a humble log cabin, the congregation now resides in what was the city's tallest building from the date of its completion in 1924 until 1930. The First United Methodist Church stood firm about remaining in the city, despite the fact that many churches sold pricey downtown real estate and fled to the suburbs after World War I, and it boasts a diverse and welcoming membership.

Address 77 W Washington Street, Chicago, IL 60602, +1 (312) 236-4548, www.chicagotemple.org | **Getting there** Subway to Washington Station (Blue Line) or Washington/Wells (Brown, Orange, Pink, and Purple Line) | **Hours** Daily 7am–7pm. Free guided tours Mon–Sat 2pm & Sun after each worship service | **Tip** Is it a pigeon? A skeleton? A hungry insect? An Afghan hound? Theories abound but no one knows for sure what exactly Picasso intended to portray with his iconic, unnamed, 50-foot-tall steel sculpture, located just across the street from the main entrance to the Sky Temple.

92 The Smoke-Filled Room

Power brokering at the Blackstone

Late into the wee hours of June 11, 1920, after a disappointing, deadlocked convention at the Chicago Coliseum, a small group of U.S. senators gathered to arrange the nomination of Warren G. Harding as Republican candidate for president, in Room 404 of the Blackstone Hotel. When the deal was done and the door to the room opened, a United Press reporter noted that Harding had been officially chosen "in a smoke-filled room" and a new political phrase was officially coined. "Smoke-filled room" has referred to power boss brokering behind the scenes ever since.

If the Blackstone Hotel could talk, oh the stories it would tell! For decades, it was the place to see and be seen in Chicago. Everyone from Rudolph Valentino to Joan Crawford, and from Truman Capote to Tennessee Williams has strutted through the Beaux Arts lobby. Best known for hosting 12 U.S. presidents, from Teddy Roosevelt to Jimmy Carter, the hotel was built in 1909 at a cost of $1.5 million ($26.2 million today) and named after Timothy Blackstone, a Chicago politician, railroad executive, and founding president of the Union Stock Yards. From the storied secret passageway that JFK allegedly spirited through to visit the room of Marilyn Monroe, to the ballroom where the top stars of entertainment, including Dizzy Gillespie, Jay McShann, and Johnny Griffin, once filled the air with all that jazz, 20th-century history has unfolded in this charming, elegant hotel, a true, polished Chicago gem, still flawless after all these years.

You can still check into the Smoke-Filled Room, one of the Blackstone's most inviting suites, but leave your cigars at home. With its exquisite, French-inspired décor, formal foyer, dining and powder room, the historic, once smoke-filled parlor centers on the original marble fireplace and dazzles with its awe-inspiring, panoramic views of Lake Michigan and Grant Park.

Address Renaissance Blackstone Chicago Hotel, 636 S Michigan Avenue, Chicago, IL 60605, +1 (312) 447-0955, www.blackstonerenaissance.com | Getting there Subway to Harrison (Red Line) | Tip The Blackstone also has a connection to the Chicago mob. Al Capone was a frequent guest of the in-hotel barbershop, appreciative of the fact that the barbershop had no windows. Now converted into a one-of-a-kind meeting space, the former barbershop retains its original fountain element, and you can still spot the traces of the original barber chairs on the marble floor. You might recognize the ballroom as the setting where Robert De Niro, playing Al Capone, beats two men with a baseball bat, in the Academy-Award-winning movie *The Untouchables*.

93_Southport Lanes

Pinspotting

There is one very important, life-saving (or at least leg-saving) rule that needs to be followed at Southport Lanes: don't bowl if you see legs. That's because here the pins are still reset and cleared, and your bowling ball still returned, by "pinboys," real people who work behind the scenes.

Southport Lanes was originally known as the Nook, a "tied house" built by the Schlitz Brewery sometime around 1900. Tied saloons were required to buy their beer from one specific brewery. See if you can spot the globe motif, tied with a red Schlitz belt, on the building's northern façade. When Prohibition hit, the tavern transformed into a more "multipurpose" venue: a speakeasy with a convenient upstairs brothel and four bowling lanes were all established to keep the money flowing, while the billiards room of today served as an illegal gambling parlor with direct lines to horse racetracks across the country. Ask the bartender to show you the dumbwaiter – concealed today behind the bowling shoe cabinet – that was once used to bring refreshments up to the working ladies.

Southport Lanes is the antithesis of the modern bowling alley. The sport here is slow, easy, and hand scored. The pinspotters were never replaced by modern automation, so you'll need to cool your heels while they do their work.

You can also opt to play classic billiards or candlepin, a variation of bowling popular in New England that calls for smaller balls and thinner pins – no pun intended. The original mural above the ten pins, with its lovely ladies dancing and frolicking around a globe, might subliminally persuade you to go with a good old can of Schlitz, but nowadays there are also 32 craft beers on tap for you to choose from now.

Don't forget to tip the pinspotters by sticking a dollar bill in your bowling ball's finger hole and sending it down the gutter.

Address 3325 N Southport Avenue, Chicago, IL 60657, +1 (773) 472-6600, www.southportlanes.com | **Getting there** Subway to Southport (Brown and Purple Line) | **Hours** Mon–Thu 4pm–2am; Fri noon–2am; Sat noon–3am; Sun noon–1am | **Tip** Further down Southport, yet another glorious Schlitz globe on the western façade marks Schuba's past life as a Schlitz tied house. Today it is considered one of the best small music venues in Chicago, thanks to a diverse line-up of live music seven nights a week (3159 N Southport Avenue, +1 (773) 525-2508, www.schubas.com).

94 South Side Elevated Car

Back when commuting was an elegant affair

On May 27, 1892, a six-car train carrying 300 guests rolled down 39th Street to the Congress Parkway Terminal downtown and straight into history. The South Side Elevated Railroad was the first-ever elevated rapid transit line in Chicago. Running from downtown Chicago to Jackson Park, with branches to Englewood, Normal Park, Kenwood, and the Union Stock Yards, this was the train that once shuttled fairgoers to the World's Columbian Exposition from May 1 through October 30, 1893. Much of the route that this train once rambled down is still used today as part of the iconic Chicago L system.

Though today the train is frozen in its tracks, you can still step aboard L Car No. 1 at the Chicago History Museum, where it has been lovingly restored and now welcomes passengers going nowhere. It took two days to relocate the 42,000-pound car, which had been gathering dust at the CTA's storage facility, very carefully, and then cautiously lift it into the second floor of the museum.

CTA riders today will feel like they are entering another world altogether as they step into this posh car. Pulled by steam locomotives, with doors on both ends of the car, the interiors that once greeted the city's commuters were luxurious by today's standards, complete with fine, varnished wood, ornate gas lighting, and rattan seats. The South Side Elevated Railroad provided 24-hour service, a boon to the city that works day and night. People had previously relied on cable railroads, which required daily overnight shutdown for cable maintenance.

Short for "Elevated", the Chicago L is the second-oldest rapid transit system on the continent after Boston's, and a visit to Chicago isn't complete without a ride around the Loop on the L. Though the cars have changed over the years, stepping up and onto the Brown Line at Adams and Wabash still gives a timeless perspective of Chicago from its elevated tracks.

Address Chicago History Museum, 1601 N Clark Street, Chicago, IL 60614, +1 (312) 642-4600, www.chicagohistory.org | Getting there Subway to Sedgwick (Brown and Purple Line) | Hours Mon–Sat 9:30am–4:30pm (Tue until 7:30pm); Sun noon–5pm | Tip Don't miss the Chicago History Museum's Sensing Chicago exhibit, which gives visitors the opportunity to ride a high-wheel bicycle, hear the Great Chicago Fire, smell the Union Stock Yards, and transform into a giant Chicago-style hot dog.

95_Steelworkers Park

Steel dreams

U.S. Steel provided the framework for everything from the soaring Willis Tower to the iconic steel drawbridges and even the Picasso sculpture on Daley Plaza. Founded by J. P. Morgan and attorney Elbert H. Gary in 1901, it was once the largest steel producer in the world as well the first billion-dollar corporation. The former South Works manufacturing plant on Chicago's Southeast Side, which opened in the late 1880s and was controlled by U.S. Steel by the turn of the century, took advantage of the fresh water and easy shipping that both the adjacent Lake Michigan and Calumet River provided. African-American migrants from the south and immigrants from around the world flooded the area, eager to work in the growing steel industry. When the plant shut down permanently in 1992, the vacant space and its crumbling remains were a sad reminder of the city's shifting economy. In 2014, Steelworkers Park rose from the ashes of the South Works and was dedicated to the many workers who provided the steel frames that made Chicago rise from the prairies to the skies.

As you wander the 16.5-acre Steelworkers Park, a slice of nature in the city, it can be hard to imagine that the South Works located on this same site for over a century once employed over 20,000 workers. Yet the park is dotted with reminders, including a series of enormous concrete ore walls, now vacant storage buildings, and even a rusting crane that marks the mouth of the Calumet River. Flowers grow where molten steel once flowed. A sweeping vista of Lake Michigan and the city skyline built by U.S. steel provide a beautiful backdrop.

Southeast Side artists Roman Villarreal and Roman DeLion created the proud statue at the park's entrance depicting a hard-hat-wearing steelworker and his family. A plaque reads "Tribute to the Past. To all the union men and women and their families who shared the steel dreams."

Address E 87th Street at Lake Michigan, Chicago, IL 60617, +1 (312) 747-6651, www.chicagoparkdistrict.com/parks | **Getting there** Train to 87th Street (Metra Electric Line) | **Hours** Daily 6am–11pm | **Tip** Steelworkers Park is popular with breeding prairie and scrubland birds, and local birders. Be on the lookout for rare birds such as the western kingbird, northern mockingbird, black-billed cuckoo, grasshopper sparrow, great black-backed gull, orchard oriole, and Bell's vireo during the summertime.

96__Taj Sari Palace

Bollywood dreamin'

Bollywood dreams come true at Taj Sari Palace on Devon Avenue, in the heart of Chicago's Desi Corridor. Enter this small boutique in your drab wardrobe, and you'll leave dressed in a bright, multi-colored, embellished sari, with rhinestone-studded drop earrings flowing from your earlobes and armfuls and armfuls of brilliant bangles.

You'll feel as if you've landed in New Delhi as you walk along this bustling, ten-block stretch of Devon Avenue, which runs from Ravenswood to California Avenues. It is one of the best-known and largest South Asian communities of its kind in North America, and the astounding variety of ethnic shops, cafés, and restaurants to be found along the avenue make it a unique, multicultural travel destination within the city. Try to pay a visit when Chicago's "Little India" is at its liveliest during the parades for India and Pakistan's Independence Days, both in August, and the night before Ramadan ends, when fireworks and festivities abound.

Taj Sari Palace's sales staff will be happy to help you find the perfect sari for your next dressy occasion. If you're looking for inexpensive, ultra-comfy yet highly unique casualwear, a fine selection of tunics or *kurtis* serve as the perfect accompaniment to your favorite pair of stretchy pants. A rainbow of silk, wool, and pashmina shawls and scarves rounds out the accessory selection. Taj Sari Palace also boasts a wide array of jewelry, including billions of bangles. Wrap up your new look with a self-adhesive, bedazzled *bindi*.

Despite the fact that Taj Sari Palace is a female-focused boutique, men will be happy to note the assortment of elegant *kurtas*, which are loose, elegant shirts that fall either just above or somewhere below the knees.

Taj Sari Palace, like many other Desi Corridor shops, welcomes and even expects bargaining, so get ready to make a deal.

Address Address 2553 W Devon Avenue, Chicago, IL 60659, +1 (773) 338-0177, www.tajsaripalace.com, tajsareepalace@hotmail.com | **Getting there** Metra to Rogers Park, then bus 155 at Morse & Glenwood to Devon & Rockwell | **Hours** Wed – Mon 11am – 8pm | **Tip** Tahoora Sweets & Bakery (2345 W Devon Avenue, Chicago, IL 60659, www.tahoora.com) features an unparalleled selection of mouthwatering South Asian treats. Try the delightful *falso*, small pink and white balls of specialty cheese bathed in sugar syrup.

97__Taylor Street Bocce Courts

A match made in Italy

Nestled between storefronts and apartment buildings, across from the Conte di Savoia grocery store (1438 W Taylor Street), *bocce* players both curse and cheer one another on in *Italiano* as they play a game that has its origins in ancient Rome. The stakes are high on these two public *bocce* courts, and anyone is welcome to take a gamble and give the game a try at any time of the day.

Taylor Street is the main drag that crosses through the beating heart of Chicago's own Little Italy. Once home to a larger, close-knit Italian-American community, the 1961 decision to build the University of Illinois and the construction of the Eisenhower Expressway and the University of Illinois at Chicago Medical District forced many of the residents to disperse throughout the city and suburbs, causing Little Italy to be greatly diminished.

Many families have returned to the area in recent years as it has rapidly gentrified, and today Chicago's Little Italy, anchored by Our Lady of Pompeii church, remains a vibrant hub of Italian-American culture, with Taylor Street at the center of the action.

Matches here begin when a randomly chosen team of two, three, or four, or even a single player, throws a jack – a smaller ball, a.k.a. *pallino* – from one end of the court into a zone 16 feet in length that ends 8 feet from the far end of the standard-sized court. After the *pallino* is successfully thrown, teams take turns trying to get their *bocce* as close to it as possible. All balls must be thrown underhanded.

You'll need to bring your own set of balls to play at these off-the-radar courts. Games tend to get quite heated, so plan on cooling off with an Italian lemonade from nearby Mario's (1066 W Taylor Street). Even better, sit back on one of the benches, relax, sip your *limonata* and watch the games unfold on a spring afternoon, when the courts hop with the best *bocce* players this side of Rome.

Address Located in the passageway across the street from 1438 W Taylor Street, Chicago, IL 60607 | Getting there Subway to Polk (Pink Line) | Tip Fuel up post-match with a sub sandwich from Conte di Savoia. Bring a picnic basket, and they will pack it to the brim with Italian-style sandwiches, snacks, desserts, and a bottle of wine (1438 W Taylor Street, +1 (312) 666-3471).

98 The Tiffany Dome

Grand souvenir of the Gilded Age

Featuring over 30,000 pieces of glass in 243 sections embraced within an ornate cast-iron frame, the Chicago Cultural Center's Tiffany Dome is the largest in the world of its kind. This splendid souvenir of Chicago's magnificent Gilded Age almost magically changes color as natural light pours through its stained-glass panels.

The Tiffany Glass & Decorating Company exhibition at the 1893 World's Columbian Exposition in Chicago launched the newly formed firm onto the international stage, leading to a number of important commissions in Chicago and beyond. Installed in the center's Preston Bradley Hall in 1897, the grand dome was designed by Jacob Adolphus Holtzer, an artist who made his mark with his elegant, electrified lantern, the precursor of the Tiffany lamp, also exhibited at the World's Columbian Exposition.

The dome's Tiffany Favrile glass, cut in the shape of fish scales, colored stones, and mother of pearl elements, was all fabricated in Tiffany's New York studio by the Women's Glass Cutting Department, headed by Clara Driscoll, a gifted Tiffany artisan who until recently was largely forgotten. The signs of the zodiac circle the top. At the base, a famous quote by British Author Joseph Addison is a reminder that the Chicago Cultural Center once acted as the city's central public library: "Books are the legacies that a great genius leaves to mankind, which are delivered down from generation to generation as presents to the posterity of those who are yet unborn."

Today, the Chicago Cultural Center serves as a creative hub, showcasing the performing, visual, and literary arts. Try to visit the space on Wednesdays at 12:15pm, when the outstanding Dame Myra Hess Memorial concerts, named after the British pianist who organized some 1,700 free lunchtime concerts for Londoners during World War II, are presented free of charge under the majestic dome.

Address Chicago Cultural Center, 78 E Washington Street, Chicago, IL 60602, +1 (312) 744-6630, www.chicagoculturalcenter.org | Getting there Subway to Randolph/Wabash (Brown, Orange, Green, Pink, and Purple Line) | Hours Mon–Thu 9am–7pm; Fri & Sat 9am–6pm; Sun 10am–6pm | Tip The Chicago Cultural Center's Sidney R. Yates Gallery, originally the library's main reading room, is a replica of an assembly hall in the Doge's Palace, Venice. The gallery's lavish interior surfaces were also created by the Tiffany Glass & Decorating Company.

99_Trephined Skull Exhibit

Appreciation for modern medicine

For anyone looking to have chills sent up their spine, the International Museum of Surgical Science delivers. The exhibits here deal with various aspects of Eastern and Western medicine. How were procedures, some that are easily carried out today – circumcision, bone repair, enemas, elephantiasis of the prostate reduction – conducted in the past? Founded by Dr. Max Thorek in 1954, this small but fascinating and somewhat ghastly museum will have you cringing in imaginary pain while simultaneously thanking God for modern medical advances.

The exhibits are displayed by theme or surgical discipline, with a focus on ailments once difficult to manage but easily treated today. Of striking interest is the trephined skull exhibit, located at the top of the stairs on the fourth floor. These timeworn skulls painfully illustrate trepanation, the archaic, misguided practice of drilling a hole into the skull to expose the *dura mater*, and thus relieve migraines, epilepsy, mental disorders, and other ailments, or to remove bone fragments from a head injury, while also assuring the release of any bad spirits dwelling within the body, and ending unusual behaviors in their unwitting host. Whether or not the people that once claimed these skulls as their own survived their trepanation is unknown, but ancient skulls show a reasonable level of healing.

Other items of note on display include an ancient Roman era enema syringe, an intact iron lung, an 18th-century self-propelled wheelchair, a Civil War-era bone saw, a turn-of-the-century hemorrhoid removal kit, kidney stones found in Egyptian mummies from the 28th Dynasty, and ancient Egyptian tablets depicting circumcision.

The museum itself is housed in a 1917 mansion designed as a Chicago-style interpretation of the Petit Trianon of Versailles. Ask the front desk attendant to show you the original, gilded elevator.

Address International Museum of Surgical Science, 1524 N Lake Shore Drive, Chicago, IL 60610, +1 (312) 642-6502, www.imss.org | **Getting there** Subway to Sedgwick (Brown and Purple Line) | **Hours** Tue–Fri 10am–4pm; Sat & Sun 10am–5pm | **Tip** Head to the reconstructed turn-of-the-century apothecary and see if you can spot the various bottles of Lydia E. Pinkham's tonic remedies: these once wildly popular, fanciful potions, which promised to alleviate "female complaints," contained herbals but also a helpful percentage of alcohol.

100_Tribune Tower Façade

Fragments of history

In 1922, the Chicago Tribune newspaper hosted a high-stakes, international design competition for its new headquarters, offering a whopping $100,000 in prize money to the winning architect. Two hundred and sixty entries poured in from around the world. The winning design, drafted by New York architects John Mead Howells and Raymond Hood, called for a neo-Gothic skyscraper complete with gargoyles, buttresses, and a crown inspired by Rouen Cathedral in Normandy, France. The stunning cathedral of journalism soared to a height of 462 feet into the sky by the time it was completed in 1925, launching the Tribune as a large, important, and international newspaper housed in "the most beautiful office building in the world," the goal of owner and publisher Colonel McCormick. Reflecting this ambition is the fascinating and distinctive façade, which is encrusted with 150 fragments from historically important sites around the world.

Who gathered all the significant fragments from the four corners of the Earth? The tradition began in 1914 when McCormick himself was on assignment in Ypres, Belgium. He took time out from covering WWI and toured a medieval cathedral that had been damaged by German shelling. He pocketed a piece of the building and carried it home to Chicago. The Tribune's other foreign correspondents followed suit, bringing back rocks and bricks from their journeys. The various fragments were incorporated into the façade, giving visitors the chance to touch history, literally. All the major sites in the world are represented, from the Great Pyramid to the Great Wall, from Notre Dame de Paris to the Palace of Westminster. The tradition continues to this day. More recent embedded artifacts added to the collection include a sample from the Sydney Opera House, and a steel remnant of the World Trade Center towers destroyed during the September 11, 2001 terrorist attacks.

Address 435 N Michigan Avenue, Chicago, IL 60611 | **Getting there** Subway to Grand (Red Line) | **Tip** One artifact was considered too precious to place on the building's exterior façade: a fragment of the Cave of the Nativity in Bethlehem appears on an interior wall inside the lobby.

101 Tuberculosis Sanitarium

A breath of fresh air

North Park Nature Village, with its loop leading through wetlands and open prairies populated with deer, is a wonderful place to catch a breath of fresh air in the city. Most of the people happily hiking its trails don't realize that once upon a time, the 46-acre nature preserve served as a lifesaving facility for up to a thousand patients suffering from a deadly disease.

Tuberculosis was a leading cause of death within the city of Chicago at the turn of the 20th century. The urban poor were hit especially hard. Widespread concern led to the passage of the Glackin Tuberculosis Law in 1909, and a special property tax was dedicated to treatment and control. In 1915, the city built the Chicago Municipal Tuberculosis Sanitarium, the largest municipal sanitarium in the country, a 650-bed, 32-building facility that provided short- and long-term care and treatment at no cost to unfortunate city residents suffering from often fatal TB.

The many windows, and walkways surrounding the building, demonstrate the theory that fresh air was vital for treating TB. Female patients lived in the brick cottages at the south section of today's village; the north section was reserved for men. A research facility was housed in the current Peterson Park Fieldhouse; the nature village's main lodge served as the dispensary. Today senior citizens occupy the former cottages, and only small clues indicate the sad history of this corner of Chicago: the graphic symbol of human lungs with a medical cross appears on several façades.

Mortality rates from tuberculosis declined slowly in Chicago in the early 20th century thanks to new drug therapies that controlled the disease effectively. The city planned to turn the waning hospital into a shopping center and apartments; thankfully, the neighborhood organized to transform the property into the peaceful nature oasis that it is today.

Address North Park Village Nature Center, 5801 N Pulaski Road, Chicago, IL 60646, +1 (312) 744-5472, www.chicagoparkdistrict.com | Getting there Subway to Irving Park (Blue Line) then CTA bus 53 to Pulaski & Ardmore | Hours Daily 10am–4pm | Tip The annual Maple Syrup Festival, hosted every March at the North Park Nature Village, taps into trees planted for the sanitarium over a century ago, and features storytelling, crafts, and a demonstration of the maple-syrup-making process via bonfire.

102_Turtle Racing at Big Joe's

May the reptilian odds be ever in your favor

The betting is always exciting at Big Joe's "tracks." Every Friday evening at 9pm, this Lincoln Square dive bar plays host to one of the most unique, high-jinx races in the city. Six turtles compete against one another in a raucous, reptilian race to the finish. Which is the fastest turtle in town? When the turtles hit the tracks here, it is guaranteed to be an extremely slow "dash" to the finish line.

Here is how it works. Arrive early and drink lots of beer. Pitchers here run at just $8. With each pitcher of beer, you will receive raffle tickets for a chance to become an official turtle jockey. An emcee will announce the winning numbers for six turtle races throughout the night plus a special grand finale race, so don't give up, and keep drinking up to increase your turtle odds. If your number is called, you get to pick your lucky turtle from the crew of feisty competitors and head to the racing arena.

The starting point of these particular races is the center of a pool table: the turtles line up, with a cake lid covering them to prevent any false advances. Once the cake lid is lifted, the turtles race at top turtle speeds to the finish line, which is actually the edge of the pool table. Your job as jockey is to cheer your turtle on with all your might. Just don't expect this race to be a quick one.

The turtles here live their lives in the lap of luxury. Well cared for in their deluxe habitat, they are also indulged with love by both the staff and bar regulars. Spend more than one Friday night cheering them on, and you will get to know their unique names and personalities – and athletic prowess. The best part of these slow-as-molasses races is that even losers are winners. If your turtle makes it to the finish line first, you'll win a T-shirt. If you're turtle is the last one to make a move, or never makes a move at all, you'll win a free drink on the house.

Address 1818 W Foster Avenue, Chicago, IL 60640, +1 (773) 784-8755 | **Getting there** Subway to Damen (Brown and Purple Line) | **Hours** Sun–Fri 1pm–2am; Sat noon–3am | **Tip** Chicagoans love a good bar competition. Streeterville Social (455 N Park Drive, +1 (312) 840-6600), a swanky rooftop bar in the Lowes Chicago Hotel, hosts life-sized Jenga competitions in the summertime. And all bets are on at Sluggers World Class Sports Bar (3540 N Clark Street, +1 (773) 248-0055), located a stone's throw from Wrigley Field, where batting cages greet baseball and beer loving patrons.

103 Union Stock Yard Gate

Hog butcher for the world

In 1865, a group of railroad companies acquired a 375-acre swathe of swampy land on the South Side of Chicago, creating the Union Stock Yard & Transit Co., known more commonly as the Yards. By 1870, 2 million animals had been butchered in the meatpacking district that made Chicago "hog butcher for the world." By the start of the 20th century, 25,000 employees were passing through the entrance gate to the Yards, where they worked under miserable conditions to produce 82 percent of the meat consumed across the US. The Yards were easily accessible to all railroads serving Chicago, and the enormous stockyard was receiving over 12 million cattle and hogs by 1890.

Journalist and novelist Upton Sinclair spent seven weeks working undercover here; his 1906 exposé *The Jungle* revealed the horrific sanitary and working conditions of Chicago's meatpacking industry, including dreadful tales of men falling into vats of boiling lard, diseased cattle being transformed into canned meat and rats accidentally winding up in sausages. Sinclair famously noted, "They use everything about the hog except the squeal." These graphic descriptions led in 1906 to the passage of the federal Pure Food and Drug and Meat Inspection Act, which in turn led to the development of the Food and Drug Administration. The meatpackers eventually formed unions, demanding better working conditions and fair compensation.

Designed around 1875 by John Wellborn Root of Burnham and Root, the limestone Union Stock Yard Gate was commissioned by the superintendent of the Yards, John B. Sherman. Over the arch of the gate is a bust of "Sherman," the beloved, prize-winning bull of this Stock Yard boss and co-founder.

The rugged gate is all that is left of the legendary Union Stock Yards, which closed following decades of decline, after over one billion animals had been processed, at midnight on July 30, 1971.

Address W Exchange Avenue at Peoria Street, Chicago, IL 60609 | Getting there Subway to Halsted (Orange Line) then CTA bus 8 to Halsted & Exchange | Tip Directly behind the gate is a memorial statue for the 21 Chicago firefighters that lost their lives in the 1910 Chicago Union Stock Yards Fire. The names of 530 Chicago firefighters killed in the line of duty up to 2004 are engraved around the base of the memorial.

104_ Vaudezilla

Become a burlesque bombshell

From the early 1880s until the early 1930s, Chicago played host to a hot vaudeville theater scene, where burlesque dancers performed scintillating shows. Arrests for indecent exposure were commonplace. Strippers made their names on the stage, like Sally Rand, who performed her sensational ostrich feather fan dance at the 1933 Century of Progress (and who was subsequently arrested four times in one day). Then came Prohibition, and the first nudie films, and burlesque became a thing of the past.

Enter Vaudezilla, where a new generation of sassy and sexy performers are finding their footing and bringing burlesque back to the Chicago theater scene.

Vaudezilla is an academy of all things burlesque, a place where even the most bashful babe can conquer her fears and hit the stage with a sexy act of her own. Born in 2008 when solo Chicago burlesque performer Red Hot Annie teamed up with Keith Emroll (a.k.a. Dick Dijon), the school offers classes in everything from slapstick tease, to boa dancing, to fan veil mastery. For those jonesing to give burlesque a go, Vaudezilla's Cabaret Showgirl Intensive, a series of intensive workshops that include one-on-one coaching and group exercises, completely immerses attendees in the creative process of modern burlesque. On the last Friday of the camp, attendees perform onstage for the very first time in their new burlesque persona.

"Students come to Vaudezilla expecting to learn how to dance and to feel sexy in their own skin while they do it, and our burlesque classes accomplish that," explains owner Red Hot Annie. "But the thing I hear over and over again is how empowering it is to embrace yourself in class and onstage. Confidence, taking up space, and the ability to hold the attention of a room are skills that apply to everything from personal relationships to public speaking, and they are skills you can learn through burlesque."

Address 3330 W Irving Park Road, Chicago, IL 60618; +1 (773) 558-0081, www.vaudezilla.com | Getting there Subway to Belmont (Blue Line) | Hours See website for class schedule and upcoming special events. | Tip Vaudezilla also hosts a number of free community events each month, including the popular Craft and Crab sessions, the burlesque version of a "Stitch and Bitch," where you can drop by with your latest work in progress to chat, vent, and make new friends while working on your costume.

105 Vavoom Pinups

Meet your retro self

If you've ever dreamed of traveling back in time and meeting a retro version of yourself, Vavoom Pinups is a time machine that will introduce you to your more glamorous, pinup alter ego. This full service photography studio will transform you from modern woman to vintage bombshell and then capture the moment in a sassy, sexy photoshoot.

When owner Heather Stumpf was about 10, sitting at her grandfather's drafting table, she came across some old pinup illustrations printed on cards in one of his drawers. Fascinated by the bombshells' beautiful curves coupled with wide red-lipped smiles on their faces, little did she know that her life's passion had just been born. "I'm a firm believer that we are all beautiful as women," declares Stumpf. "Each one of us deserves to feel iconic, timeless, and glamorous. Empowerment starts from within, but when you add the Vavoom experience, it explodes!"

When you arrive at the studio you'll trade your 21st-century duds for a sexy, silk robe. Vavoom's team of hair and make-up stylists will bring out your retro best. Then choose a new outfit, shoes and accessories from the endless closet of vintage finery. Then choose your background from a complete 1950s mint green and yellow kitchen set, a mod carpeted living room set, or even a tiki bar.

"Our clients are physically and emotionally empowered through each part of the process. Most of us haven't seen a photo of ourselves from head to toe ... and when you do it's exciting, and for many women the experience is eye-opening," gushes Stumpf. "So many of our clients come back and tell us how Vavoom 'changed them' how the experience 'took them to the next level' in their own lives. Women who, after their shoot, could finally find their voice, who took that trip they always wanted, or were just ready for the next challenge. If that isn't empowering ... I don't know what is!"

Address 724 W Hubbard Street, Chicago, IL 60654, +1 (773) 726-1109, www.vavoompinups.com | Getting there Subway to Grand (Blue Line) | Hours By appointment | Tip The stylists at Tigerlilie Hair Salon are specialists in the long-lost art of real vintage hairdressing. From pixies to beehives, they can make your retro hair dreams reality (4539 N Western Avenue, +1 (773) 506-7870, www.tigerlilie.com).

106_Vienna Beef Hot Dog Factory Cafeteria

Hold the ketchup

A classic, Chicago-style hot dog is a Vienna Beef frankfurter – boiled, steamed or charred – nestled in a steamed, poppyseed bun, squirted with yellow mustard, and then "dragged through the garden" with the addition of chopped white onions, sweet pickle relish, a dill pickle spear, tomato wedges, sport peppers, and a dash of celery salt for a final zing. Don't even think about adding ketchup. The belly-filling meal for a nickel moved from pushcarts on Maxwell Street to stands across the city when Austro-Hungarian immigrants Emil Reichel and Sam Ladany sold their Vienna Beef hot dogs at the 1893 World's Columbian Exposition. Their success at the fair made it possible for the duo to open up their first Vienna Beef Hot Dogs storefront on Chicago's Near West Side at 417 S Halsted Avenue.

Not long after, wieners wrapped in buns became a hit at baseball parks, fairs, and other sporting events. By 1908, Vienna Beef hot dogs were delivered across Chicago via horse-drawn carriage; in 1928 they shifted to a motorized delivery fleet.

At the Vienna Beef Hot Dog Cafeteria you can bite into a factory-fresh hot dog with all the requisite toppings alongside the employees who make the tasty, iconic dog possible. It is not fancy, and you'll have to grab a tray and wait in line with other workers during peak lunchtime hours. But it is clean and congenial, and the hot dogs here are fresh from the source and prepared by the true masters of the weenie.

The shop in front sells house-made hot dogs by the case, as well as bulk-packaged bagel dogs, corned beef, pastrami, poppyseed buns and all the condiments you'll need for summer picnics. T-shirts, posters and other Vienna Beef goods are also available for anyone wanting to express their love of the tried and true Chicago-style hot dog.

Address 2501 N Damen Avenue, Chicago, IL 60647, +1 (773) 435-2309, www.viennabeef.com | Getting there Subway to Damen (Blue Line) then CTA bus 50 to Fullerton & Damen | Hours Mon–Fri 8am–3pm; Sat 10am–3pm | Tip The Wiener Circle is a Hot Dog Hall of Famer that serves up Chicago-style, Vienna Beef dogs, charred – with a side of verbal abuse. The servers here are notorious for slinging insults – sometimes playful, sometimes hostile – at customers, so enter with your self-confidence in check (2622 N Clark Street).

107_Walt Disney's Birthplace

Where the magic was born

In 1891, a young couple, Elias Disney and his wife, Flora, moved from Kissimmee, Florida to Chicago. Elias was a carpenter by trade, and he was able to secure a job at the World's Columbian Exposition of 1893. The couple purchased an empty lot at 2156 N Tripp Avenue, in Chicago's Hermosa neighborhood, for $700. Flora designed the home of her dreams, and, with his own two hands, Elias built the rectangular, frame home where they would add two more children to their family of four. Walter "Walt" Disney was born in the second-floor bedroom.

Younger sister Ruth followed suit two years later, completing the Disney family of seven. When Walt was just four, the family moved to a farm in Marceline, Missouri, the small town that inspired the Main Street USA at Walt Disney World.

Few people realize that this modest home was the birthplace of an American cultural icon, and for years it stood sadly in a state of disrepair. There are not any historical markers to indicate that this house was the birthplace of the Disney dream. It wasn't until the current owners, Brent Young and Dina Benadon, stepped in to save the day that the home began to breathe with new life. The duo purchased the property and has plans slowly to restore the home back to its early 20th-century glory. They also plan eventually to transform it into a multimedia-rich museum, as well as a center for early childhood creativity.

The Disney family returned to Chicago from Kansas City and settled on the Near West Side in 1917, after Elias Disney invested in the O-Zell Company, a jelly and juice producer. Young Walt attended McKinley High School and took evening cartooning classes at the Chicago Academy of Fine Arts. Walt Disney lived in Chicago until he became an ambulance driver for the Red Cross in September 1918, after which he was shipped to France, never to live in Chicago again.

Address 2156 N Tripp Avenue, Chicago, IL 60639, www.thewaltdisneybirthplace.org | **Getting there** Train to Healy Station (Metra Milwaukee District/North Line) | **Tip** Elias Disney not only built the St. Paul Congregational Church (known as Iglesia Evangelica Bautista Betania today), that stands at 2255 N Keeler Avenue, one block east and one block north of Walt Disney's birthplace, but also named his son after the church's pastor, Walter Parr. Walt Disney was also baptized there.

108_Wood Block Alleys

Horse-drawn days

In the early 19th century, as major American cities dreamed of addressing the issue of their muddy and unsanitary streets, Boston developer Samuel Nicolson came up with the idea of paving streets with wooden blocks. His innovation made its way to Chicago, where plentiful lumber from Wisconsin did indeed make wooden blocks a cheaper and less noisy street-paving alternative. The hooves of the city's working horses pounded slightly more softly on Nicolson's paved streets. By 1871, Chicago had 37 miles of wood-block-paved streets. You can still find three wood-paved alleys hidden throughout the city, true souvenirs of Old Chicago.

The finest example (and easiest to find) is the narrow alleyway, closed to traffic, that runs between State and Astor Streets, behind the grand Gold Coast mansion of the Archbishop of Chicago. In nearby Lincoln Park, a small east-west alley just south of Webster Avenue and west of Hudson Avenue also features well-worn blocks. Yet another tiny, hard-to-find dead-end alley on the south side of Roscoe Street, just west of Inner Drive, is also paved with wood. Close your eyes and imagine when horses, not cars, trotted along our city streets.

Nicolson pavement called for white oak or cedar blocks, four by five inches wide, and twelve to fifteen inches long, laid together loosely on the four-inch side over a sand foundation, with the spaces in between packed with a mixture of gravel and coal tar. Nicolson's innovation was short lived, however, since his wood blocks were both slippery and stinky. They also tended to decay due to moisture retention. Eventually, wood blocks were replaced with brick or Belgian blocks. Contrary to popular belief, wood pavement was chemically treated and did not burn easily; though it was reported that the streets were aflame when the Great Fire of 1871 leveled the city, most wooden-blocked streets survived.

Address Alley at the rear of 1555 N State Parkway; east-west alley just south of Webster Avenue and west of Hudson Avenue; dead-end alley on the south side of Roscoe Street, just west of the Inner Drive | **Tip** Built in 1885 at the direction of Most Reverend Patrick A. Feehan, the first Archbishop of Chicago, the historic Archbishop's Residence at 1555 N State Parkway has housed seven archbishops. Note that the mansion has two entry façades, one for pedestrians and the other for horse-drawn carriage arrivals, joined at a square corner, with entrances scaled to the streets they face.

109 World's Columbian Exposition Ticket Booth

After the fair has gone

Just 22 years after the Great Chicago Fire devastated the city, a glorious, picture-perfect "White City" rose from the ashes. American architect and urban planner Daniel H. Burnham oversaw the construction of nearly 200 grand, neoclassical buildings on more than 600 acres of land. Each stuccoed building was washed in white and illuminated with modern electric lights. Throughout the fairgrounds, gas lamps glowed, their light reflecting romantically in the many canals and lagoons. The White City was a marvelous sight to see.

But the magical White City wasn't meant to last. The grand façades were made not of marble but of staff, a mixture of plaster, cement, and jute fiber that would not survive the harsh Chicago winters for long. Shortly after the fair closed, a fire destroyed many of the buildings; the rest were torn down. Only the former Palace of Fine Arts, which houses today's Museum of Science and Industry, and the building that housed delegates to World's Congresses, today's Art Institute of Chicago, survived in their original foundation. The Maine State Building was moved to Poland Spring, Maine, and the Dutch House was brought to Brookline, Massachusetts. Few people know that one small building also survived, which can still be found in Chicagoland: an authentic World's Columbian Exposition ticket booth.

Located in the side yard of the Frank Lloyd Wright designed Hills-DeCaro House, the ticket booth is often mistaken for a garden toolshed. It has been everything from a children's playhouse to a bunny hutch. The house remains a private residence, but it is occasionally opened for special tours, and you can always sneak a peek at the booth and imagine the days when visitors to the fair excitedly paid for their tickets to the long-gone White City.

Address 313 Forest Avenue, Oak Park, IL 60302 | Getting there Subway to Harlem / Lake (Green Line) | Tip St. John Cantius Church features a main altar and two side altars that reputedly originate from the fair. The historic church was dedicated in 1893, the same year that the World's Columbian Exposition took place (825 N Carpenter Street).

110_Zap Props

Where the film industry scores its treasures

A set design coupled with the perfect props can bring your story to life on stage, in the movies, or in your very own home. Zap Props' huge 36,000-square-foot warehouse, one of the largest in the world, holds all the whimsical objets d'art, period pieces, and oddball items that film and theater directors crave. This unique depot manufactures unique props in-house and rents out modern and antique props to create the backdrop of your dreams. The store is packed from floor to ceiling with objects that will take you back in time or back to the future: disco balls, vintage bicycles, working phonographs, prop guns, mannequins, and more. Chances are you'll recognize many of the pieces, most of which have already debuted in a movie, television or stage production.

Chicago was a hub for motion picture production long before Hollywood became the home of the stars. In the early 1900s, there were more production companies and filmmakers based in Chicago than in any other U.S. city. Uptown-based Essanay Studios, best known today for its series of Charlie Chaplin comedies of 1915, produced multiple silent films every week. In the 1980s, a film production revival in Chicago led to such iconic blockbusters as *The Blues Brothers*, *Sixteen Candles*, *Ferris Bueller's Day Off*, *The Color of Money*, *Risky Business* and *The Untouchables*. A 30 percent tax credit on all film production costs within the state of Illinois, established in 2009, brought filmmakers back to Chicago.

Zap Props is the go-to spot for the film industry in Chicago, and owner Bill Rawski and his team also offer in-house printing and framing, as well as a full wood and welding shop, making it easier to customize or create one-of-a-kind design elements. Rawski himself has no idea exactly how many objects are in his endless, continuously-evolving inventory, making a trip to Zap Props a true treasure-hunting experience.

Address 3611 S Loomis Place, Chicago, IL 60609, +1 (773) 376-2278, www.zapprops.com | Getting there Subway to Ashland (Orange Line) | Hours Mon–Fri 9am–6pm | Tip Before Chicago's dismal winter weather sent the movie stars out west, Essanay Studios produced silent films with such stars as Colleen Moore, Gloria Swanson, and of course Charlie Chaplin. Studio co-owner G. M. Anderson starred in the very popular *Broncho Billy* westerns. Though the studio stopped production, you can still visit the Essanay Film Manufacturing Company building at 1345 W Argyle Street.

111 Zebra Lounge

Still swinging after all these years

An outstanding night on the town always ends at the Zebra Lounge, sipping lemon drops and singing with the piano man into the wee hours. Hidden in the lobby of a vintage apartment building in the glam Gold Coast, the Zebra Lounge has been swinging with live music seven nights a week since 1929.

It wasn't until millionaire real-estate magnate and hotelier Potter Palmer moved to the area in 1882 that the Gold Coast transformed from down-and-out swamplands to one of the swankiest spots in the city. Though Palmer's 43-room castle met the wrecking ball, the area retains its posh exclusivity. While Division Street is the home to many rowdy, college-kid populated bars, the Zebra Lounge, hidden on elegant State Parkway, is where the area's more seasoned residents cap the night with one last cocktail before tucking into bed.

Look for the discreet, black-and-white Zebra Lounge sign on the bottom left corner of the Canterbury Court façade on swanky State Parkway, and enter via the foyer. The zebra motif pops up everywhere in the intimate, safari-friendly interior: zebra lamps illuminate the bar, zebra-inspired art lines the walls, black and white stripes keep the cocktail menu in check. The 45-seat room starts swaying at around 10pm, when the lounge's signature martinis and bubbling champagne have hit the spot, and the music starts inspiring new friendships and loves.

People come to the Zebra Lounge for the piano men, a rotating crew of five piano entertainers who play all the classics, with "Piano Man," and "Fly Me to the Moon" among the top requests. An electronic keyboard tops the old Kimball piano because it is easier to amplify.

The menu at this lively lounge lists solely champagne, wine, beer, and three signature martinis, including the must-try Faster Pussycat, with its premium tequila, Grand Marnier, splash of Chardonnay, and fresh lime wedged along a salted rim.

Address 1220 N State Street, Chicago, IL 60610, +1 (312) 642-5140, www.thezebralounge.net | Getting there Subway to Clark/Division (Red Line) | Hours Mon–Fri 6pm–2am; Sat 7pm–3am; Sun 7pm-2am | Tip Scenes from the 1986 hit movie *About Last Night*, starring Rob Lowe and Demi Moore, were shot at Mother's. The heart sign above the door lets Division Street passersby know that this bar is a place to meet a sweetheart, if only for the night (26 W Division Street).

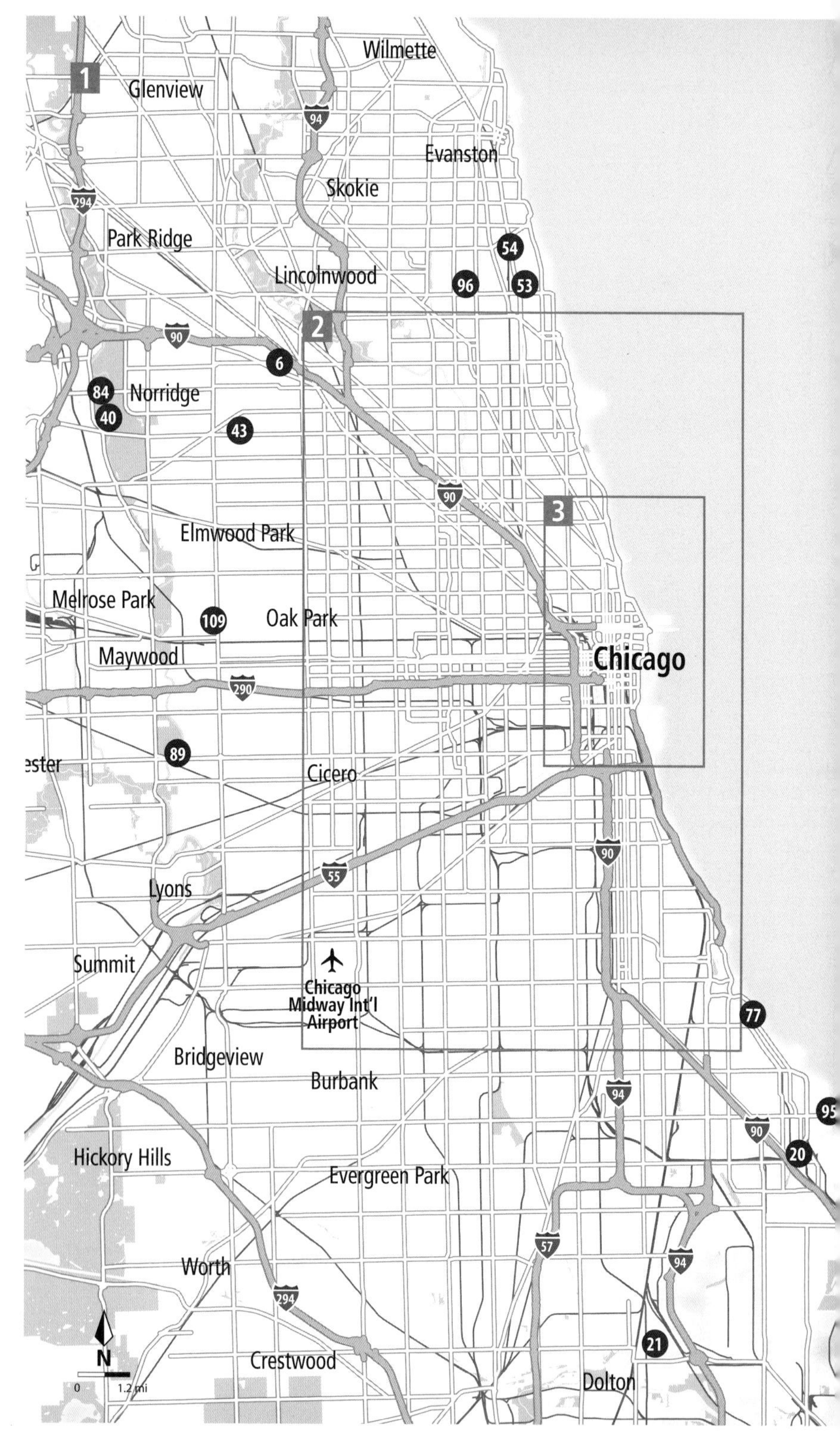

Wilmette
1
Glenview
94
Evanston
Skokie
294
Park Ridge
54
Lincolnwood
96
53
2
90
6
84
Norridge
40
43
90
3
Elmwood Park
Melrose Park
109
Oak Park
Chicago
Maywood
290
89
Cicero
90
55
Lyons
Summit
Chicago
Midway Int'l
Airport
77
Bridgeview
Burbank
94
95
90
20
Hickory Hills
Evergreen Park
57
94
Worth
294
N
21
Crestwood
0
1.2 mi
Dolton

2
3
W Peterson Ave
N Western Ave
N Pulaski Rd
W Lawrence Ave
W Irving Rd
N Elston Ave
N Milwaukee Ave
N Cicero Ave
N Ashland Ave
W Belmont Ave
W North Ave
W Grand Ave
Chicago
S Western Ave
S Pulaski Rd
S Halsted St
S State St
W 31st St
S Cottage Grove Ave
W Garfield Blvd
W 63rd St
Chicago
Midway Int'l
Airport
N
0
0.6 mi
94
90
290
55
101
12
102
16
42
60
3
7
63
86
59
9
37
75
38
104
87
93
72
27
5
106
4
14
73
26
107
85
19
2
48
11
83
82
24
39
13
97
45
79
44
31
76
17
110
103
47
64
66
70
15
32
71
65
57
52
33

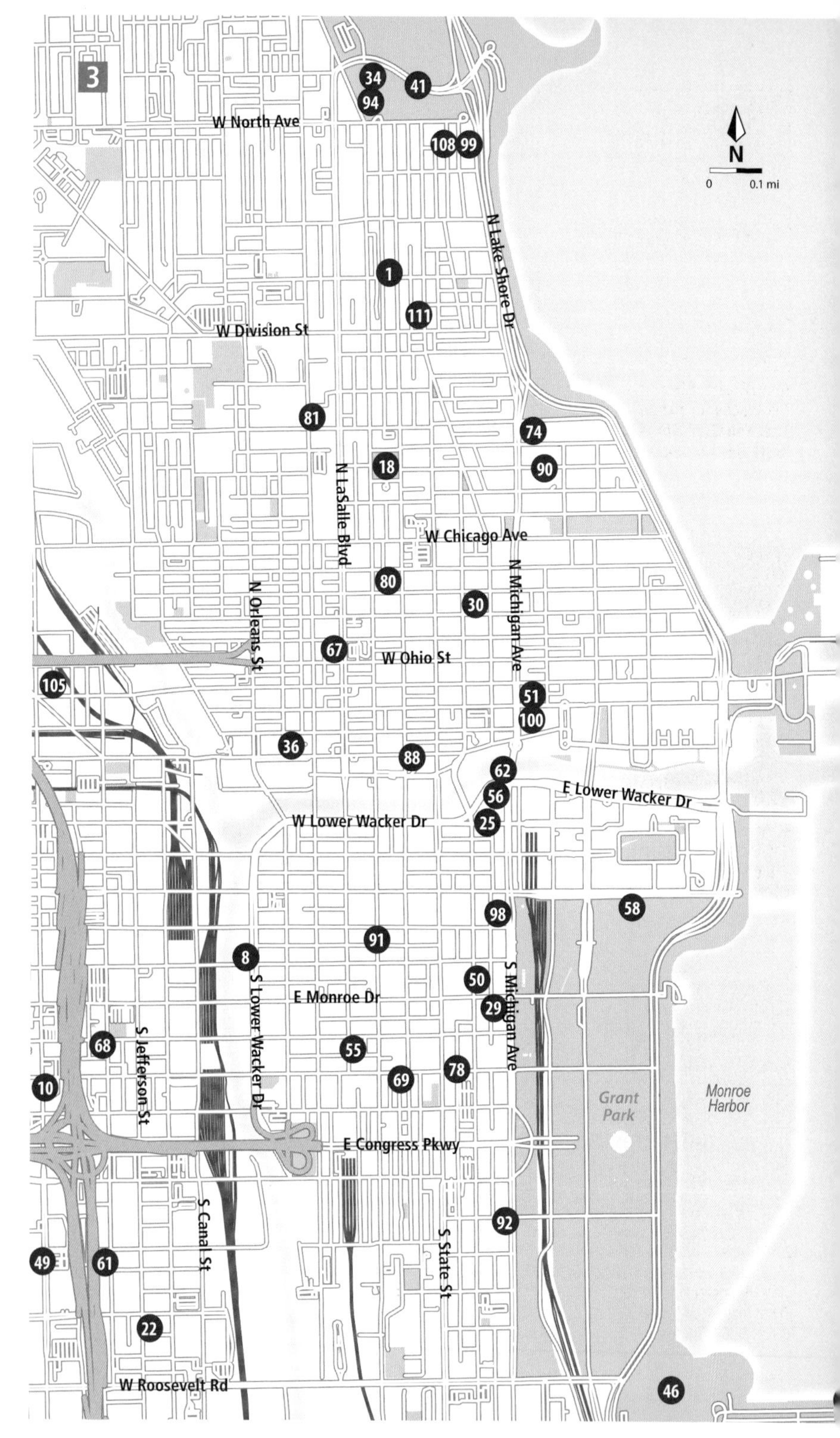
3
N
0
0.1 mi
W North Ave
W Division St
N LaSalle Blvd
N Lake Shore Dr
W Chicago Ave
N Orleans St
N Michigan Ave
W Ohio St
E Lower Wacker Dr
W Lower Wacker Dr
S Lower Wacker Dr
E Monroe Dr
S Michigan Ave
S Jefferson St
Grant Park
Monroe Harbor
E Congress Pkwy
S Canal St
S State St
W Roosevelt Rd
34
41
94
108
99
1
111
81
74
18
90
80
30
67
105
51
100
36
88
62
56
25
98
58
91
8
50
29
68
55
78
69
10
92
49
61
22
46

Amy Bizzarri, Susie Inverso
111 Places for Kids in Chicago
That You Must Not Miss
ISBN 978-3-7408-0599-9

Michelle Madden, Janet McMillan
111 Places in Milwaukee
That You Must Not Miss
ISBN 978-3-7408-0491-6

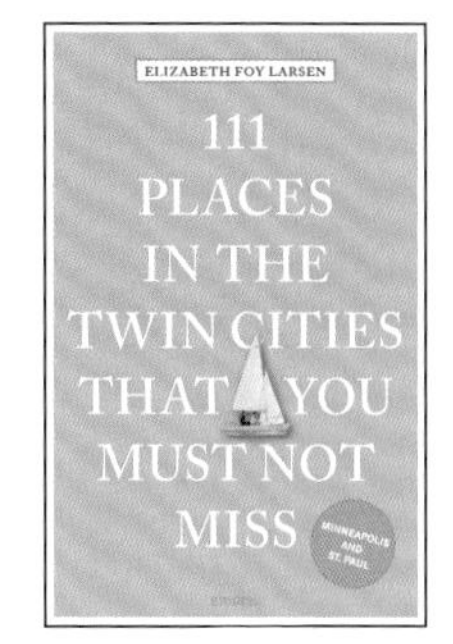

Elisabeth Larsen
111 Places in the Twin Cities
That You Must Not Miss
ISBN 978-3-7408-0029-1

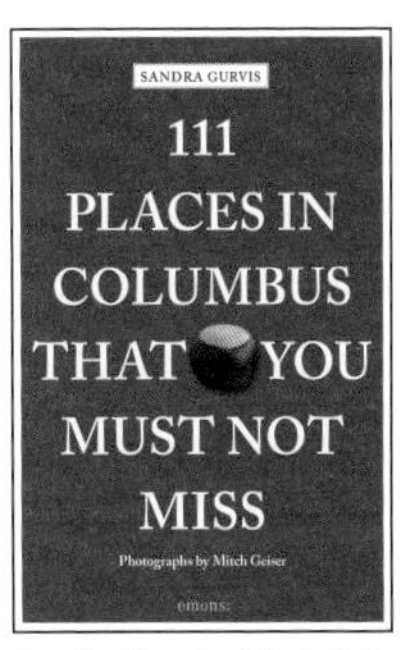

Sandra Gurvis, Mitch Geiser
111 Places in Columbus
That You Must Not Miss
ISBN 978-3-7408-0600-2

Kelsey Roslin, Nick Yeager,
Jesse Pitzler
111 Places in Austin
That You Must Not Miss
ISBN 978-3-7408-0748-1

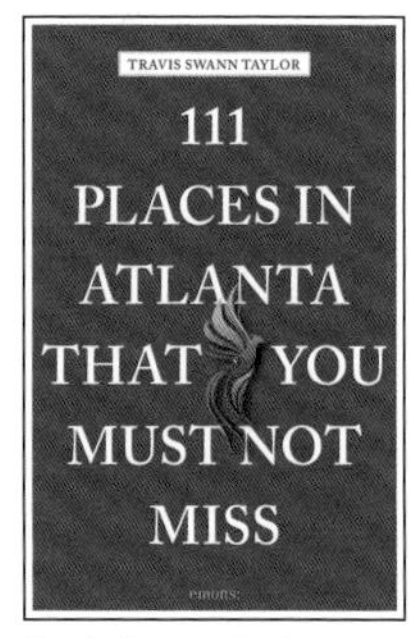

Travis Swann Taylor
111 Places in Atlanta
That You Must Not Miss
ISBN 978-3-7408-0747-4

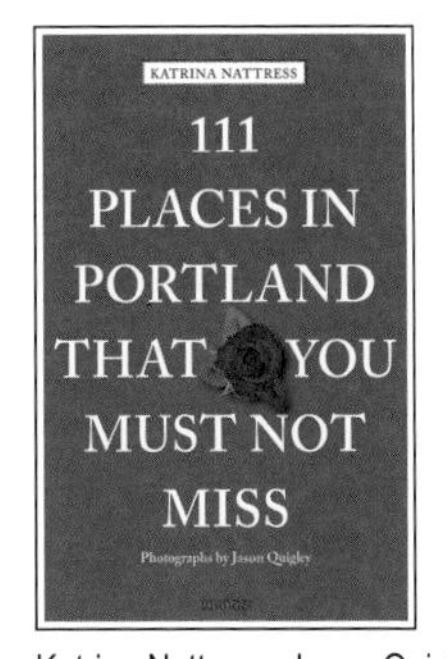

Katrina Nattress, Jason Quigley
111 Places in Portland
That You Must Not Miss
ISBN 978-3-7408-0750-4

Floriana Petersen, Steve Werney
111 Places in Silicon Valley
That You Must Not Miss
ISBN 978-3-7408-0493-0

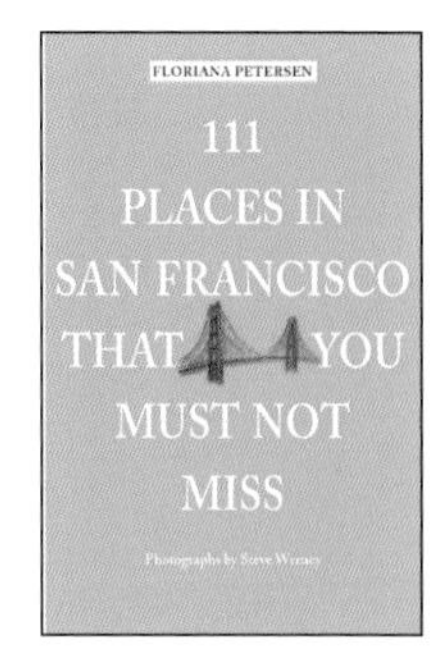

Floriana Petersen, Steve Werney
111 Places in San Francisco
That You Must Not Miss
ISBN 978-3-95451-609-4

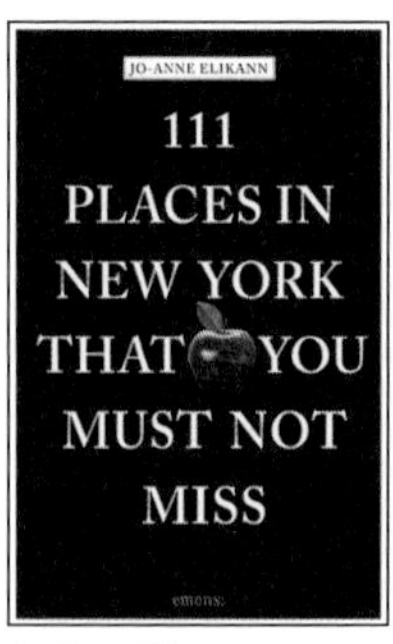

Jo-Anne Elikann
111 Places in New York
That You Must Not Miss
ISBN 978-3-95451-052-8

Wendy Lubovich, Jean Hodgens
111 Places in the Hamptons
That You Must Not Miss
ISBN 978-3-7408-0751-1

Wendy Lubovich, Ed Lefkowicz
111 Museums in New York
That You Must Not Miss
ISBN 978-3-7408-0379-7

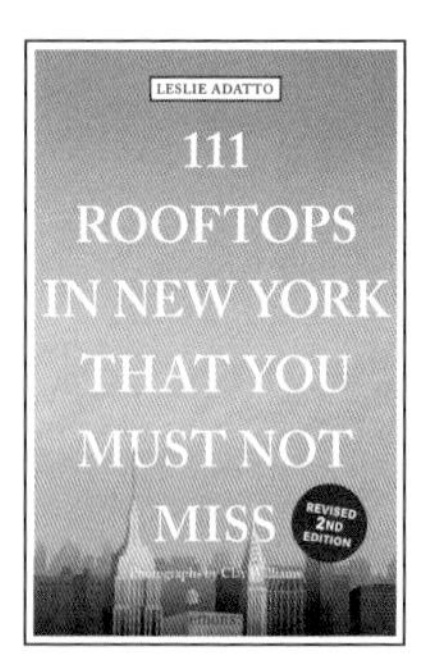

Leslie Adatto, Clay Williams
111 Rooftops in New York
That You Must Not Miss
ISBN 978-3-7408-0495-4

John Major, Ed Lefkowicz
111 Places in Brooklyn
That You Must Not Miss
ISBN 978-3-7408-0380-3

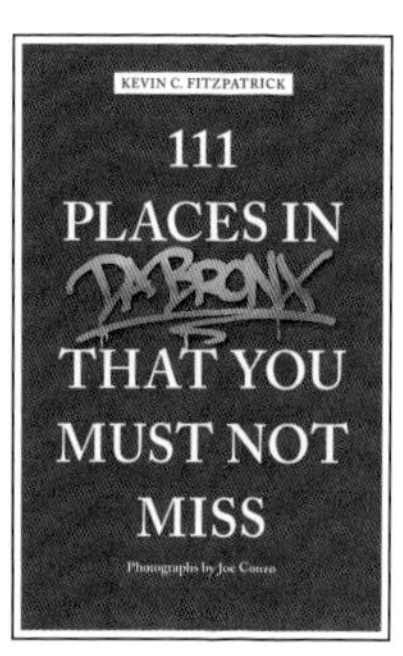

Kevin C. Fitzpatrick,
Joe Conzo
111 Places in the Bronx
That You Must Not Miss
ISBN 978-3-7408-0492-3

Joe DiStefano, Clay Williams
111 Places in Queens
That You Must Not Miss
ISBN 978-3-7408-0020-8

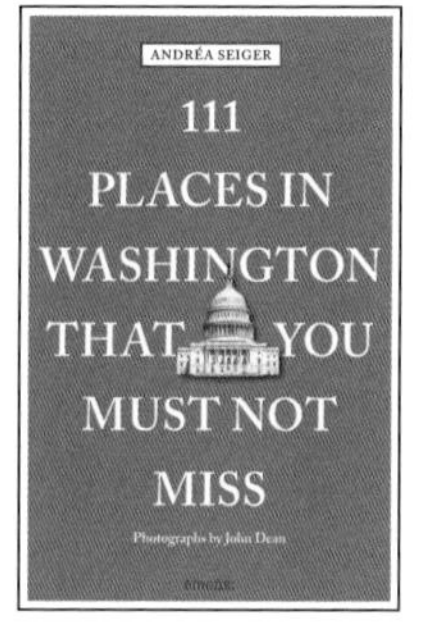

Andréa Seiger, John Dean
111 Places in Washington
That You Must Not Miss
ISBN 978-3-7408-0258-5

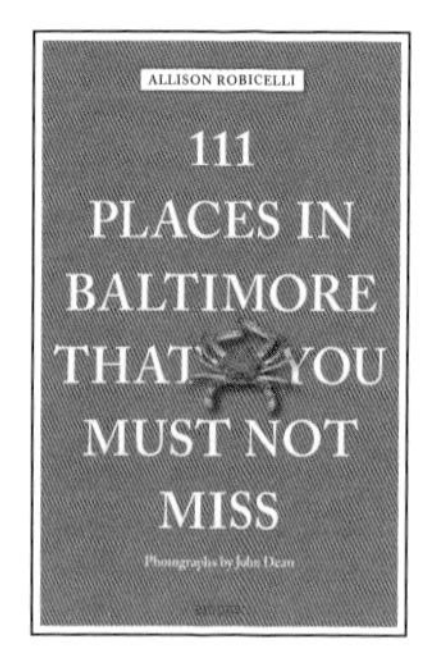

Allison Robicelli, John Dean
111 Places in Baltimore
That You Must Not Miss
ISBN 978-3-7408-0158-8

Gordon Streisand
111 Places in Miami and the Keys That You Must Not Miss
ISBN 978-3-95451-644-5

Dave Doroghy, Graeme Menzies
111 Places in Vancouver That You Must Not Miss
ISBN 978-3-7408-0494-7

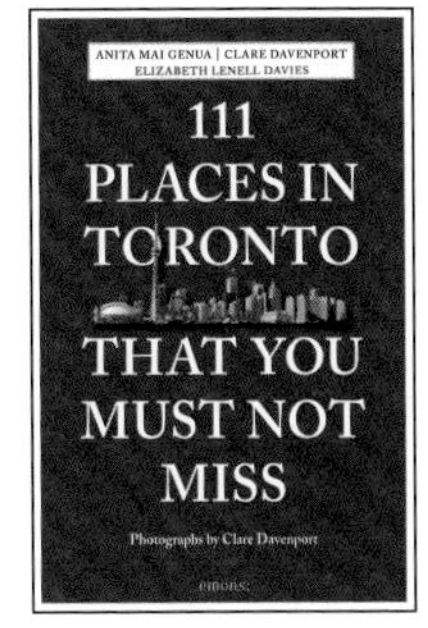

Anita Mai Genua,
Clare Davenport,
Elizabeth Lenell Davies
111 Places in Toronto That You Must Not Miss
ISBN 978-3-7408-0257-8

Benjamin Haas, Leonie Friedrich
111 Places in Buenos Aires That You Must Not Miss
ISBN 978-3-7408-0260-8

Beate C. Kirchner,
Jorge Vasconcellos
111 Places in Rio de Janeiro That You Must Not Miss
ISBN 978-3-7408-0262-2

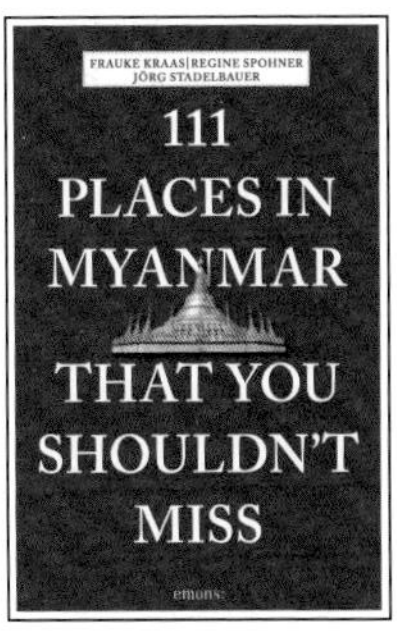

Frauke Kraas, Regine Spohner,
Jörg Stadelbauer
111 Places in Myanmar That You Shouldn't Miss
ISBN 978-3-7408-0714-6

Christoph Hein, Sabine Hein
111 Places in Singapore That You Shouldn't Miss
ISBN 978-3-7408-0382-7

Christine Izeki, Björn Neumann
111 Places in Tokyo That You Shouldn't Miss
ISBN 978-3-7408-0024-6

Kathrin Bielfeldt,
Raymond Wong, Jürgen Bürger
111 Places in Hong Kong That You Shouldn't Miss
ISBN 978-3-95451-936-1

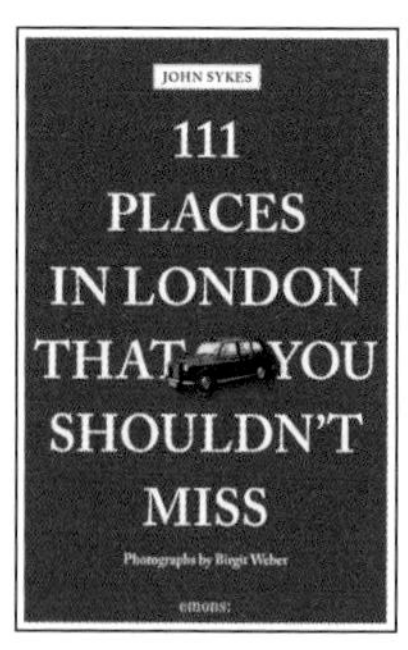

John Sykes, Birgit Weber
111 Places in London That You Shouldn't Miss
ISBN 978-3-95451-346-8

Frank McNally
111 Places in Dublin That You Must Not Miss
ISBN 978-3-95451-649-0

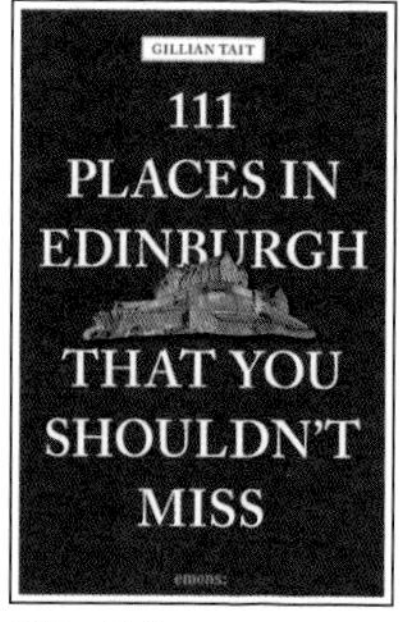

Gillian Tait
111 Places in Edinburgh That You Shouldn't Miss
ISBN 978-3-95451-883-8

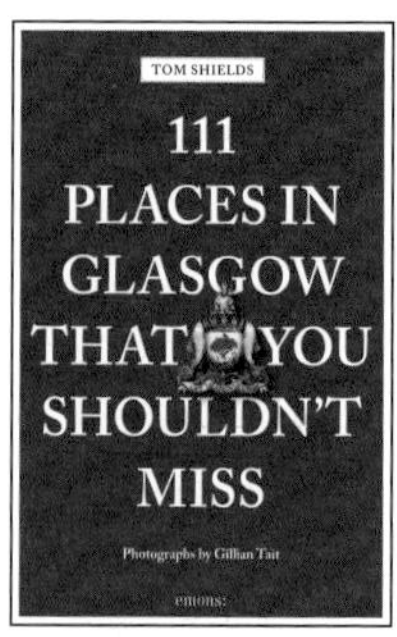

Tom Shields, Gillian Tait
111 Places in Glasgow That You Shouldn't Miss
ISBN 978-3-7408-0256-1

Kai Oidtmann
111 Places in Iceland That You Shouldn't Miss
ISBN 978-3-7408-0030-7

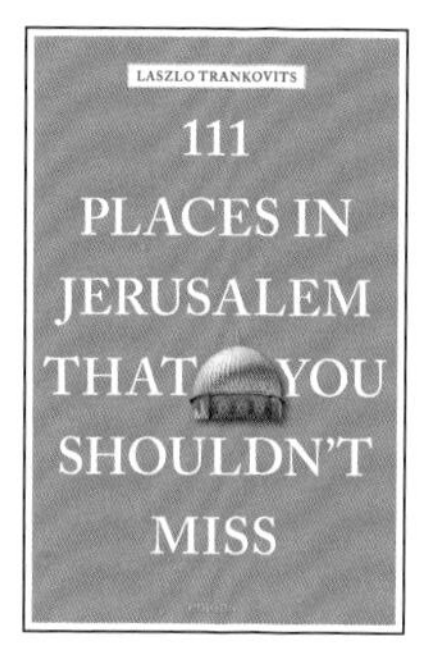

Laszlo Trankovits
111 Places in Jerusalem That You Shouldn't Miss
ISBN 978-3-7408-0320-9

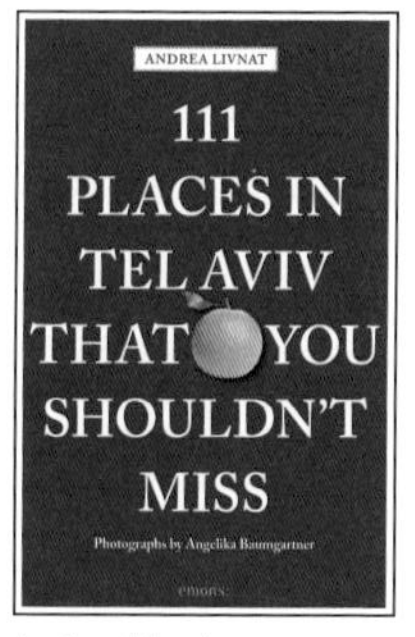

Andrea Livnat, Angelika Baumgartner
111 Places in Tel Aviv That You Shouldn't Miss
ISBN 978-3-7408-0263-9

Fabrizio Ardito
111 Places in Malta That You Shouldn't Miss
ISBN 978-3-7408-0261-5

Sybil Canac, Renée Grimaud, Katia Thomas
111 Places in Paris That You Shouldn't Miss
ISBN 978-3-7408-0159-5

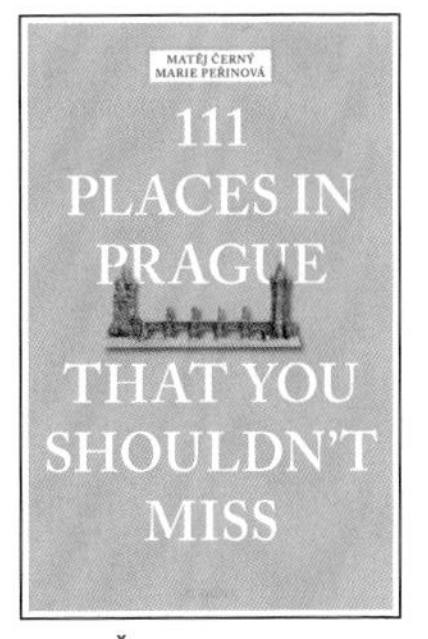

Matěj Černý, Marie Peřinová
111 Places in Prague
That You Shouldn't Miss
ISBN 978-3-7408-0144-1

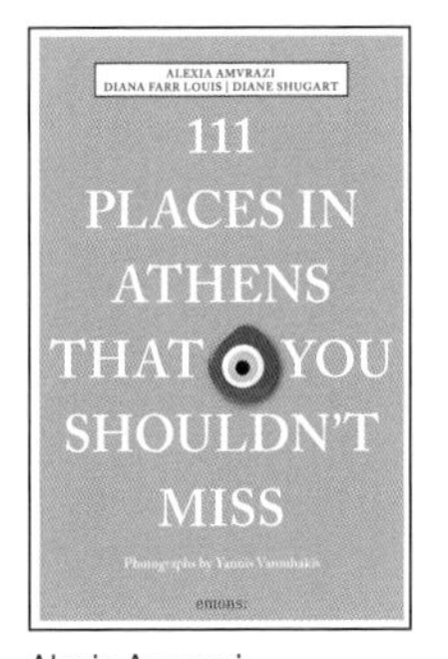

Alexia Amvrazi,
Diana Farr Louis, Diane Shugart,
Yannis Varouhakis
111 Places in Athens
That You Shouldn't Miss
ISBN 978-3-7408-0377-3

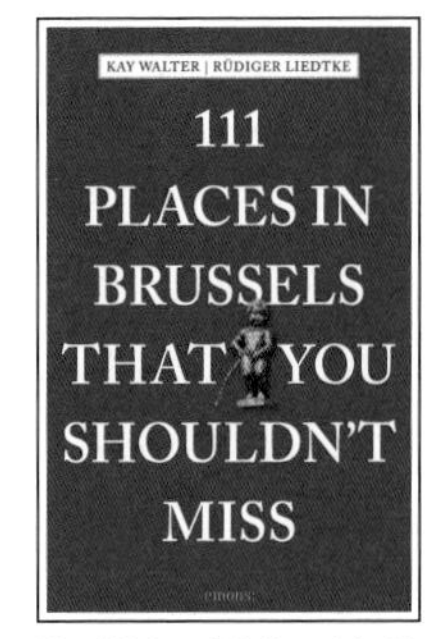

Kay Walter, Rüdiger Liedtke
111 Places in Brussels
That You Shouldn't Miss
ISBN 978-3-7408-0259-2

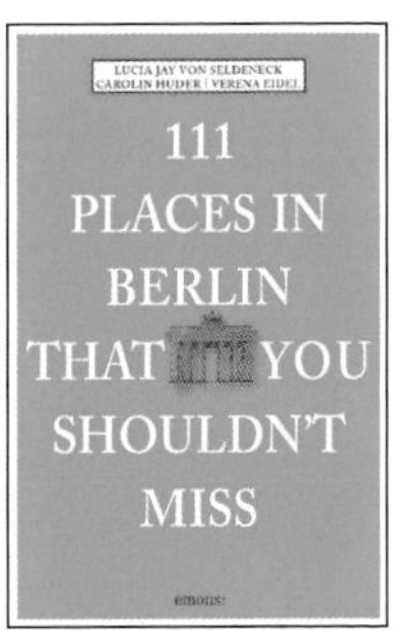

Lucia Jay von Seldeneck,
Carolin Huder
111 Places in Berlin
That You Shouldn't Miss
ISBN 978-3-7408-0589-0

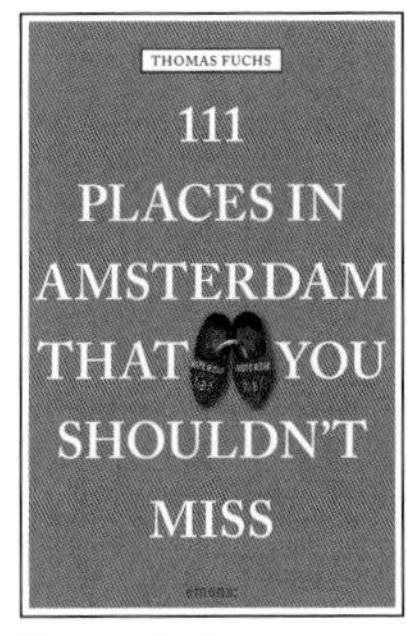

Thomas Fuchs
111 Places in Amsterdam
That You Shouldn't Miss
ISBN 978-3-7408-0023-9

Kathleen Becker
111 Places in Lisbon
That You Shouldn't Miss
ISBN 978-3-7408-0383-4

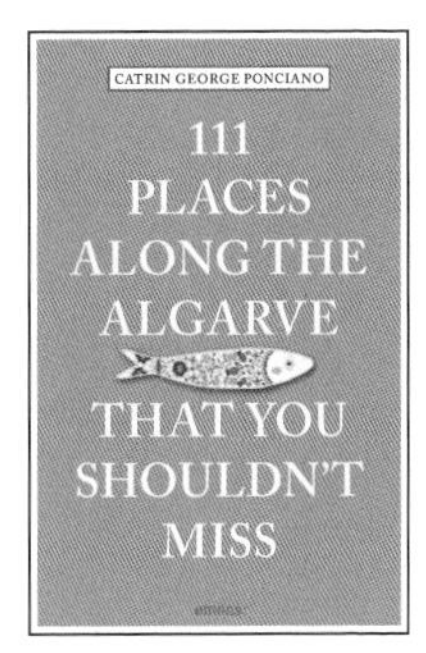

Catrin George Ponciano
111 Places along the Algarve
That You Shouldn't Miss
ISBN 978-3-7408-0381-0

Annett Klingner
111 Places in Rome
That You Must Not Miss
ISBN 978-3-95451-469-4

Dirk Engelhardt
111 Places in Barcelona
That You Must Not Miss
ISBN 978-3-95451-353-6

Acknowledgements

A galaxy of thanks goes to my husband, Justin, for encouraging me to do what I love, and to his family who allowed me to drag them around Chicago on a beautiful March day (one of the few!) to complete the photography of the outdoor locations.
– *Susie Inverso*

Amy Bizzarri is an extreme Chicago-history buff and freelance writer. She lives with her two children in a vintage 1910 home in the Logan Square neighborhood of Chicago. When she's not writing, you'll most likely find her swimming laps at Holstein Park pool, riding her bicycle around Humboldt Park or sharing an atomic sundae at Margie's Candies.

Susie Inverso has spent many years running around Chicago photographing the CTA public transit system, and photographs weddings and portraits for her company, Crimson Cat Studios. When she's not photographing trains, people, or pets, she plays the trumpet and guitar in various musical projects, and enjoys road trips with her husband, Justin. They live on the North Side with their two cats and box turtle.